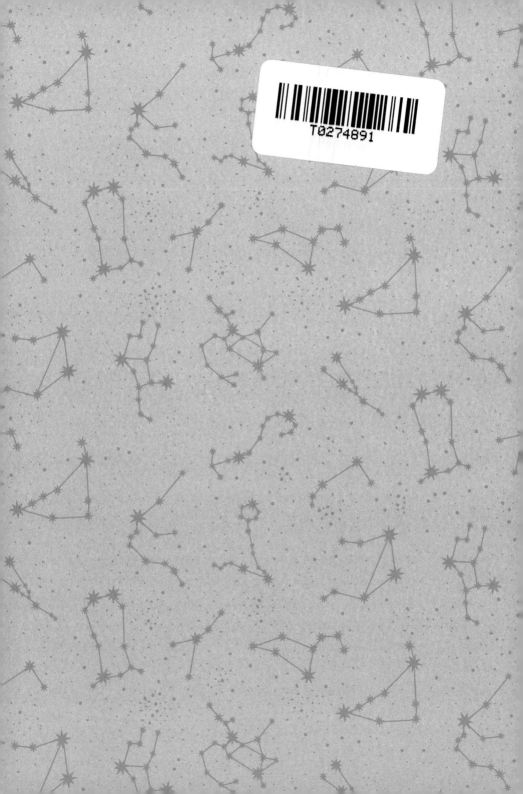

T0274891

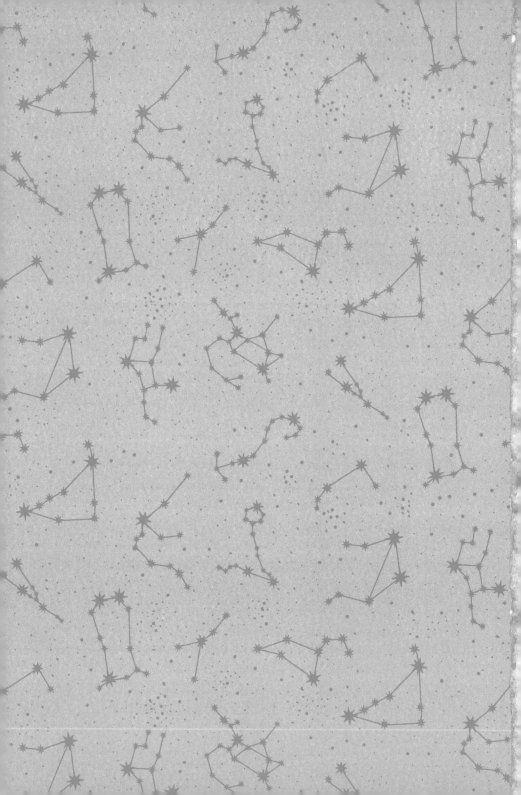

Praise for *Astrology Decoded*

"Vish has an otherworldly ability to bend time with his teachings. The depth of his ancient Vedic wisdom combined with his practical and futuristic understanding of humanity will guide you toward a quantum leap forward in living your soul's purpose."

—Devi Brown, well-being educator, media personality, and author of
Crystal Bliss: Attract Love. Feed Your Spirit. Manifest your Dreams.

"I absolutely love this book. Vish harnesses his scientific background to dispel doubt, giving us permission to trust in the genius of Vedic astrology. In clearly written, beautifully designed pages, this book makes this divine gift of knowledge easy to understand and practical for all. I will be recommending it to all my clients and students!"

—Laura Plumb, Ayurvedic practitioner; yoga, Ayurveda, and Vedic astrology teacher;
and author of *Ayurvedic Cooking for Beginners*

"Over the centuries, various aspects of India's ancient wisdom—yoga, meditation, Vedanta philosophy, Ayurvedic medicine—moved from the fringes of Western society into the mainstream. What was once considered antiquated became seen as rational and practical. Quite possibly, the same will be true of Vedic astrology, which can be remarkably accurate and predictive in the right hands. This astute and sensible book makes a valuable contribution to that process."

—Philip Goldberg, author of *American Veda: From Emerson and the Beatles
to Yoga and Meditation: How Indian Spirituality Changed the West*

"Astrology Decoded is an excellent guidebook for understanding Vedic astrology and applying it to your life. Together, the planets, houses, and zodiac constellations create a unique sketch of your transpersonal psychology, which you can apply to health, business management, relationships, and vocational guidance. In this book, Vish has seamlessly blended his knowledge of yoga, Ayurveda, and Vedic astrology with his own formidable analytical skills. Astrology Decoded is a modern-day take on Vedic counseling that can empower people to transform their lives."

—Dr. Suhas Kshirsagar, BAMS, MD (Ayurveda), best selling author,
motivational speaker, and Ayurvedic physician

"Astrology Decoded is an excellent title for this especially useful primer on Vedic astrology. Chatterji uses his engineer's mind to adroitly unpack the essential meaning of the enigmatic planets and signs. His explanations are specific, sophisticated, and actionable. Even the cryptic Rahu/Ketu become understandable, given his insightful contemporary treatment. And the quick reference guide is great! As a former Western astrologer, I often use the analogy of Western astrology being like a photograph versus Vedic astrology being like an MRI. This book will help students thoroughly understand these archetypal codes, allowing them to move forward, dipping their toes further into the ocean of Vedic astrology. Highly recommended!

—Professor Charlotte Benson (Jyoti Devi), president of the American College of Vedic Astrology and president emerita of the Arizona Society of Astrologers

"The journey to self-development begins with truly knowing who you are. Unlike any other leadership and personality assessment tools, this book offers a deeply personal exploration to discover your unique qualities and the gifts you bring to the world. Insightful, soulful, and packed with powerful stories that will inspire you and guide you toward unleashing your full potential in both your professional and personal lives."

—Doy Charnsupharindr, executive coach, leadership educator, and CEO of the Berkeley Executive Coaching Institute

"Vish Chatterji's brilliant new text, Astrology Decoded, provides the reader with a lucid roadmap to understand the profound astrological system of India. His writings bring this ancient, esoteric framework into a modern Western context, and his chapter on remedial measures provides practical insights for holistic healing. I predict Vish's profound book will become the cornerstone of any Vedic astrology library!"

—Dennis M. Harness, PhD, counseling psychologist, president emeritus of the American College of Vedic Astrology, and author of The Nakshatras: The Lunar Mansions of Vedic Astrology

"In this accessible and captivating work, Vish Chatterji uses his East-meets-West perspective to take the reader on a truly memorable journey through the cosmos. Astrology Decoded presents Vedic astrology in a manner that balances the basic with the mythic, the historical with the metaphorical, and the practical with the spiritual. Chatterji's expertise shines through as he makes the case that anyone interested in astrology should take a closer look at India's science of the stars."

—Drew Thomases, PhD, chair of the Department for the Study of Religion at San Diego State University, and author of Guest is God: Pilgrimage, Tourism, and Making Paradise in India

"This book does exactly what is says—it decodes astrology! The way Vish communicates the theory, mythology, and archetypes is truly beautiful. I have been taken back in time and now understand the backstory of the planets and the qualities that influence who we are today. I couldn't put this book down; each chapter left me thirsty for more knowledge about this highly sophisticated zodiac system, even as I journeyed further into my own self-discovery. Vish is a natural teacher, and he is clearly passionate about his subject. He has woven together a rich tapestry of ancient wisdom, storytelling, and deep awareness of Vedic astrology, and he has done what is often impossible—grounded it for the modern world. From my perspective as a master coach, leveraging Vedic astrology is an excellent tool for understanding your true self."

—Gillian McMichael, ICF Master Certified Coach, founder of Full Circle Global, and author of *Coming Home: A Guide to Being Your True Self*

"It was a pleasure to read such a masterwork on Vedic astrology. This book emphasizes the importance of the rising sign and explains how Vedic astrology calculations match the observed positions of planets in the sky, unlike Western astrology. Astrology Decoded is an easy read for beginners, explaining planets and signs and how one can attain karmic balance through remedies and rituals. The knowledge presented in this book is instrumental in laying a solid foundation for readers to understand the higher secrets of astrology and to unravel the play of the cosmos in day-to-day life."

—Aditya Togi, PhD, astronomy researcher and lecturer at Texas State University

"Astrology Decoded is a must-read for those seeking to transcend the limitations of mainstream Western astrology and embrace a more profound understanding of their life's journey. Vish's exploration of Vedic astrology invites readers into a transformative journey of self-discovery and spiritual insight as he illuminates the deeper dimensions of your soul's purpose, karma, and cosmic energies through captivating mythical tales and profound insights. I felt like I had a front-row seat listening to a sage sharing the stories of the ancients. This book serves as an enduring companion, guiding readers to continuously reference its wisdom throughout their exploration of Vedic astrology as it pertains to their soul's mission in this life."

—Amy Lynn Durham, executive/spiritual intelligence coach and author of *Create Magic at Work*

"In Astrology Decoded, Vish Chatterji masterfully unravels the complexities of Vedic astrology, making it accessible and relevant for our times. His approach, blending personal experiences with ancient insights, mirrors the journey many of us are on—seeking deeper understanding and harmony with the cosmos. This book stands as a beacon for those looking to navigate life's challenges with greater wisdom and purpose. It resonates with my own exploration of nature's profound

gifts and the timeless wisdom that guides us to live in harmony with it. Chatterji's work is not just informative, it's transformative, inviting us into a more aligned and purposeful way of being."

—Amish Shah, producer and director of *The Natural Law*

"Vish-ji has been practicing yoga with me for over twenty-five years, and he understands its power for personal transformation. Like yoga, Vedic astrology is an important tool for insight into one's personal karma. By understanding the planets, yogis can make informed decisions and take appropriate actions to align with their higher purpose and spiritual growth. This book offers great guidance on how to navigate challenges and obstacles on the path to self-realization."

—Yogrishi Vishvketu, PhD, Himalayan Yoga Master, founder of Akhanda Yoga, author of *Yogāsana: The Encyclopedia of Yoga Poses*, and co-author of *The Business Casual Yogi: Take Charge of Your Body, Mind, and Career*

"Vish's book is amazing and groundbreaking in so many ways! I absolutely loved reading it. It is an excellent introduction to Vedic astrology for those who have been curious about this science, as well as for long-term practitioners! Vish offers a practical understanding of the planets and their corresponding zodiac signs, including powerful remedies for those who have drifted from their true purpose. This is a foundational book for anyone interested in the vast science of Vedic astrology. I cannot recommend it enough!"

—Dr. Santhip Kanholy, Vedic astrologer/researcher and Vedic life coach

ASTROLOGY DECODED

ASTROLOGY DECODED

The Secret Science of India's Sages

Vish Chatterji, MBA

Foreword by Sheila Patel, MD
Chief Medical Officer for Chopra Global

MANDALA

SAN RAFAEL LOS ANGELES LONDON

For Chetan, Jaya, and Dharma.
May you continue to spread the light.

NAVAGRAHA MANTRA

Harih om
Navagraha devata bhyo namaha

Om adityaye cha somaye
Mangalaye buddhaye cha
Guru shukra shani-bhyas cha
Rahave ketave namaha

—Rishi Veda Vyasa, circa 3000 BCE

TRANSLATION

Salutations to the nine planets

Sun, Moon,
Mars, Mercury,
Jupiter, Venus, Saturn,
Rahu, Ketu

MEANING

We recognize the powerful influence of
the nine planets on all beings of the cosmos.
We seek their grace and blessings in our endeavors
and in finding our way back to our true selves.

Contents

FOREWORD 15

PREFACE 19

INTRODUCTION 27

CHAPTER 1
The Wisdom of the
Ancient Yogis 31

CHAPTER 2
Karma and Vedic Astrology 41

CHAPTER 3
The Nine Planets of the
Celestial Court 51

CHAPTER 4
Sun and Moon: The King
and the Queen 59

CHAPTER 5
Mars, Mercury, Jupiter,
and Venus: Members of
the Court 67

CHAPTER 6
Saturn, Rahu, and Ketu: The
Servant and the Outcastes 81

CHAPTER 7
The Vedic Sky: Your Soul's
Chart 95

CHAPTER 8
The Vedic Zodiac: The Stars That
Showered Your Arrival 105

CHAPTER 9
Finding Karmic Balance through
Remedies and Rituals 127

CONCLUSION 149

AFTERWORD 153

ACKNOWLEDGMENTS 157

QUICK REFERENCE
GUIDE 159

GLOSSARY OF
SANSKRIT TERMS 167

BIBLIOGRAPHY 173

ABOUT THE AUTHOR 175

Foreword

My introduction to Vedic astrology came when I was a child. Like Vish, I grew up hearing about my birth chart. Everyone in my family had one, and we discussed them as if we were discussing the weather—explanations for the storms in life and predictions for the atmospheric conditions ahead. It didn't seem strange to me at all.

As I grew older and developed a love for science (in the reductionist way it is taught in the West), I started asking myself questions about the "science" of astrology. Teachers and mentors talked about astrology as if it were not real, ridiculing anyone who believed in it. Throughout college, medical school, and ultimately residency, I was constantly told that astrology was magical thinking. I became so conditioned that I began to grow skeptical of the things my family valued.

During my early years as a physician, however, I often longed for a guidebook to help me better understand my patients, allowing me to choose the best treatment for them as unique individuals. I soon realized that a person's mental and emotional state had a significant effect on how disease manifests in the body—and that Western science didn't have all the answers. As I grew more curious, and a bit disillusioned, I eventually turned back toward Vedic philosophy and teachings, specifically Ayurveda, the science of life. This medical system describes various mind-body types, or constitutions, each with their own unique tendencies. Therefore, depending on the person, different treatments may be prescribed for the same disease, diagnosis, or condition.

Science is only now beginning to validate the concepts of Ayurveda (and Vedic thought more broadly), such as the importance of aligning with our circadian rhythms, the primary role of digestion in our overall health, and the interaction and connection between mind and body. These concepts were considered strange just a short while ago. As our scientific tools become more sophisticated, we may also find that there are similar explanations for the science of Vedic astrology.

Vish wrote *Astrology Decoded* to help people who are looking for a way to better understand themselves and their own unique nature. This book is an excellent reference for anyone who wants to learn the basic concepts of Vedic astrology and how it can guide their day-to-day lives. We are constantly bombarded with information for the "average" person. Needless to say, there is no average person. We are all unique, as our birth charts will tell us. When presented in an accessible voice, as Vish has brilliantly done, Vedic astrology can be used as a framework to guide our lifestyles and choices. This does not mean that we need to abandon other beliefs, practices, or treatments that are working for us. It simply means we have another tool to help us navigate the journey of life—one that can fill the gaps in those other frameworks.

I have no doubt that interest in Vedic astrology will continue grow. These teachings have been passed down through the centuries for the betterment of humanity, and the modern world is finally ready for them.

—Sheila Patel, MD, Chief Medical Officer for Chopra Global

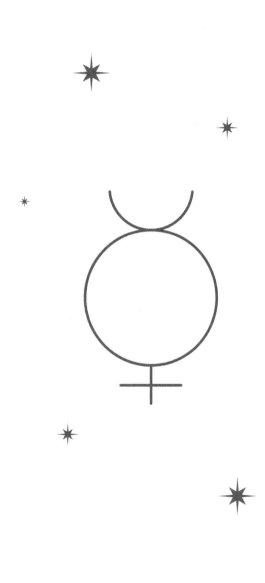

Preface

"Oh, he is such a Virgo! Since I'm a Cancer, I just don't understand him," a human resources executive explained to me at a conference as I subtly rolled my eyes. *What nonsense! That astrology stuff is all hocus-pocus!* I thought to myself, politely smiling without betraying my disdain for the subject.

Trained as a mechanical engineer and further shaped as an MBA, my rational mind endeavored to find logical explanations for everything in our universe. I maintain a healthy skepticism, testing any scientific or business thesis with hard data before drawing any kind of conclusion. My own business success in the field of product management was predicated on this data-driven approach to understanding consumer needs and market trends. To me, newspaper horoscopes, magazine astrology, and pop-culture tarot were all in the realm of make-believe. Though I had been a practitioner of yoga and meditation for over twenty years, I saw yoga as having a solid scientific and logical basis, as a sophisticated mind-body health regimen (as has been validated in recent times).

Growing up with emigrant Indian parents, yoga and the Vedic philosophy of ancient India were often discussed at family teatime and on casual Sunday mornings. But astrology was an off-limits topic at home. In the modern, educated Indian perspective, only backwater, superstitious villagers believed in "that nonsense." Reputable families such as mine, cultivated into leadership roles by generations of colonial rule, sent our kids to be educated in Western thought, science, and philosophy. We came to view the Western path to enlightened thought to be superior to the forgotten enlightened wisdom of our ancient Vedic sages. Though my family practiced our ancient rituals and festivals and talked about Vedic philosophy, outwardly we were Western in our speech, clothing, education, and career aspirations, with a firm focus on material goals over spiritual goals. Even when I was in my twenties, and backpacked in India to learn yoga, I remember my mother saying, "What will happen to his career if he runs off and becomes a yogi?"

However, there was always an undercurrent of our ancient roots beneath our outward colonial-influenced Western disposition, and one particular embodiment of this heritage lurked in my father's study.

In an outer drawer of my father's grand leather-topped cherrywood executive desk I remember a small, mysterious, and yellowing envelope labeled "Vish's Horoscope" in my mother's curly handwriting. As a child, I was told that my Vedic birth chart had been drawn up by an astrologer in India soon after I was born, but no mention of the contents was ever made. I didn't see this envelope again until some years ago, after my parents passed. The envelope surfaced within the crates of paperwork I sorted through as I settled their estate. Throughout my life, I was always afraid of what might be in this envelope; I suppose I not only thought astrology was hocus-pocus but also was fearful that it might somehow control my life or make me feel restricted in exercising my free will, a fundamental right of my Western-trained mind.

When I did finally open the envelope, forty-two years after its drafting, there emerged a 20-inch-long weathered parchment scroll, creased into folds and crammed inside. It was handwritten in Bengali script with exotic diagrams and tables, none of which I could decipher. Years went by before I was able to translate this mystical document. When it finally revealed its secrets to me, many of them turned out to be astonishingly accurate.

As the scroll indicated (to the month and year!), I first pursued an education and career in a technical field as an engineer, then I became a leader as an executive, and then I went on to start my own business. Then, as it predicted, my start-up failed and my parents got sick and eventually passed away, after which it foresaw "success, achievement and popularity" for me.

True enough, I went through an existential career crisis before finding my true calling as an East-meets-West executive coach and teacher of Vedic wisdom. During this time, I also discovered self-development parallels in the wisdom of my Indian heritage and Western leadership principles and co-wrote my first book about yoga, Ayurveda, and leadership: *The Business Casual Yogi*. In it, I recounted a performance review during my early executive days, where I received biting criticism and admonition of my hard-driving leadership style. Soon after, I came across a book on the ancient Indian mind-body medicine system of Ayurveda, another casualty of colonial suppression of indigenous wisdom. Though Ayurveda is typically employed as a healing mind-body medical system, I found wisdom in it that applied to leadership archetypes and learned ways to temper the imbalances in my fiery leadership style, eventually accelerating my executive career. This Ayurveda system categorized our psychosomatic nature into three mind-body archetypes—airy types (*vata*), fiery types (*pitta*), and earthy types (*kapha*). This framework helps us understand our natural dispositions, reactions during times of stress, and how to better balance our innate nature through lifestyle and diet changes specific to our archetype. Though typically used to understand disease tendencies and healing approaches, as I transitioned from my executive career to coaching, I adapted this model in my work to help my clients balance their own work and leadership challenges, while improving their health.

A client would come in, and I would have them take an Ayurvedic assessment quiz to identify their archetype. I would then work with them to help identify and shift leadership-limiting behaviors. However, there was one problem: Corporate culture so intently celebrates the type A personality that clients would subconsciously cheat the quiz and show up as fiery pitta types—an embodiment of their aspirational leadership goals—regardless of their true mind-body archetypes. This type-A bias in quiz results would often not align with the observable attributes and emotional disposition of the person I was seeing before me. Basically, the quiz wasn't mapping reality well when it came to executives.

During those early coaching days, I had been training in Ayurveda under my mentor, Dr. Suhas Kshirsagar, a renowned Ayurvedic physician. I brought up this leadership self-bias issue with him, and he casually explained, "Oh, you just look at their birth chart, and you will get a true read of their personality."

What? This astrology nonsense again? I thought to myself.

But I trusted in his wisdom and reputation, and in time he inducted me into the Indian Vedic system of astrology. To the satisfaction of my engineering mind, this system relied on actual positions of planets in space. I learned that some of my own skepticism around Western astrology was valid, because Western calculations of the planets and zodiac constellations weren't accurate regarding their actual positions in space, which I will delve into in the section on reality-based calculations in chapter 2.

I also discovered that the Vedic system relies on the specific location, date, and exact time of birth, versus the general month in which you were born used in Western astrology. Therefore, two people born hours apart could have very different birth charts and thus different personalities. This more accurate, person-specific approach was intriguing to me. I realized that I had applied my skepticism of Western astrology to any system that had the word *astrology* in it. I also began to realize my own negative bias toward the indigenous systems of my heritage; colonized peoples often downplay our own systems in favor of those of our colonizers. Thankfully, this personal enlightenment coincided with our current decolonization movement, where indigenous peoples all over the world are reclaiming their heritage, and as a society, we are celebrating and embracing the intelligent, universe-aligned wisdom of the indigenous medicine and healing traditions.

I began to experiment, as any scientific mind would do, asking some of my clients their birth date, exact birth time, and location. As I analyzed their horoscopes using the accurate Vedic astronomy and specific birth details, what I inferred actually lined up with the personality I was seeing before me—a ground truth and a much more accurate, unbiased understanding of the person than the Ayurvedic personality quiz could deliver. I would ask these test clients more pointed questions about their personality, and they would respond, "Wow, how do you know that about me? Very few people know that about me!"

As I saw this approach consistently give powerful personality and leadership insights, I thought to myself, *What else can I learn from a birth chart?* This began a journey into the deeper ocean of Jyotish (the Sanskrit name for the Vedic science of astrology, formally Jyotisha) and a morphing of my work into what my clients began to call Jyotish-informed executive coaching.

As I dove deeper and deeper into the system of knowledge that is Vedic astrology, I discovered a remarkably sophisticated and intelligent framework that has endured the test of thousands of years and helps explain the very meaning of our lives, careers, and relationships. It would paint an uncannily accurate picture of the strengths and weaknesses of my clients and even accurately predict when shifts would take place in their life, love, and work as my own handwritten scroll had done. Clients would remark that this system was like three-dimensional X-ray vision into their soul, as opposed to a superficial one-dimensional understanding of a part of their personality that they knew through casual Western astrology.

I began to integrate Vedic astrology into my coaching practice, where I discovered that it can help us prepare for major life events, understand the right spiritual or religious path for our mindset, choose an appropriate career, identify innate strengths and weaknesses in our character, and even identify the right leadership qualities to cultivate (as I leverage in my executive coaching work). It has enabled my clients to make more aligned decisions that support their innate personalities, talents, and abilities, often obscured by layers of constructed identities from society, family structure, educational conditioning, and yes, pop-culture horoscopes.

Furthermore, I found Vedic astrology to be fully integrated within yoga, Ayurveda, and the vast Vedic philosophy system of India—the other areas of my research, study, and practice. It was the missing piece of the eco-system I had been studying all these years; Vedic astrology is a full sister science to yoga and Ayurveda, and an equally powerful path to greater self-awareness, personal growth, and development of our deeper con-sciousness and spiritual intelligence.

Introduction

In this book, you will learn about your Vedic zodiac sign, but we must remember that we are each a combination of all the signs, because they were all present in the sky at the time of our birth. The main sign (or rising sign) influences your personality the most, but the other signs influence your personality in how you show up in various areas of your life.

Furthermore, the Vedic system sees the signs as expressions of the planets themselves, so we first need to understand the personalities of the planets, and then observe how their traits are altered through the expressions of the signs. Each Vedic sign has a planet that rules it, which defines the personality of that sign. Through knowing your Vedic sign and its planetary ruler, you can assess how you are showing up in life and whether you are aligned to the deeper innate personality that your sign would suggest. In Western astrology, I have found that one's sign doesn't always fully capture who one truly is. In the Vedic system, by using more accurate calculations, focusing on a Vedic sign specific to your birth, and understanding the condition of the planet that rules your sign, you will discover a zodiac interpretation more tailored to you, along with insights on how to improve your life.

Each sign's expression of personality depends on how strong or weak the planet ruling that sign is. For instance, you may show up as a balanced version of that sign, or in the case of an overly strong planet, an exaggerated version of that sign, or for a weak planet, a repressed version of that sign. (Note that any planets located in your Vedic sign can also influence how that sign shows up, which we will cover). Rather than requiring a professional astrologer to analyze those strengths, by learning about the personalities of the planets, you can identify how they are showing up in your life. You can train yourself to better observe the planets' energies at play, and therefore understand how to manage and improve those energies. This is especially important when it comes to the planet that rules your Vedic rising sign.

In the Vedic system, the planet that rules your rising sign becomes the lord of your entire birth chart and is a highly important planet to be aware of for a more soul-aligned life. Depending on how strong or weak that planet is, we can identify how aligned you are to your innate soul personality. So rather than blindly accepting or rejecting your zodiac sign, we are trying to discover the innate personality of your soul, and then, based on the strength of the planet that rules that sign, assess how aligned or misaligned you are in life. By knowing your innate, soul-level personality, you can then start to favor its natural tendencies, strengthening the planet that rules it. By leaning into your soul personality, you strengthen your entire chart and life.

In this book, I will start with an overview of the body of ancient Indian wisdom, from which Vedic astrology emerges, and then compare its concepts to the more popular Western astrology. I will introduce the nine planets used in the Vedic system: the Sun and Moon (which are treated as planets), followed by Mars, Mercury, Jupiter, Venus, and Saturn, and ending with two eclipse nodes of the Moon known as Rahu and Ketu. I will paint a picture of their captivating personalities through mythological stories and share how their personalities shift depending on the signs they manifest through. As you learn about your own Vedic sign, you will begin to recognize how the planetary personalities are showing up in your own life and the lives of people around you. You will then be able to determine whether you or others are showing up as strong or weak versions of the innate personality of their souls. When you learn how to tune in to and manage the energies of the planets, Vedic astrology becomes a powerful self-improvement system.

I will wrap up the book by giving you specific methods and practices to improve your soul-alignment and therefore your overall life.

Let us now tune in to a deeper understanding of our true nature.

CHAPTER 1

The Wisdom of the Ancient Yogis

"But you're a yogi! Why do you follow Western astrology instead of the astrology of the yogis?" I quizzed a yoga teacher friend in Portugal. She replied with a sly smile, "Well, I've read about Vedic astrology, but I like the Western system better because it supports my ego. I'm still attached to my ego identity, and I'm not ready to know about the truth of my soul just yet!"

This exchange puzzled me. What is the draw to Western astrology when it seems to be such a casual and superficial look at who we are? As a yogi myself, who is eternally exploring a soul-aligned life, I describe Western astrology as a photograph of your constructed ego at a given point in time, whereas Vedic astrology gives you that X-ray insight into the depths of your soul.

We have an intense attachment to the ego-formed image of ourselves, which has been further colored by the Western zodiac sign we identify with, referenced in newspapers, magazines, and social media. I began to appreciate the identity crisis my clients face when they first learn about their Vedic birth chart, which focuses on a different zodiac sign. Western astrology typically uses the position of the Sun when you were born against the backdrop of the twelve zodiac constellations encircling the sky relative to Earth. Therefore, for everyone born during a certain monthlong period, the Sun, as viewed from Earth, appears in front of a specific constellation, determining one's zodiac Sun sign.

Note that both systems agree that there are twelve primary constellations and, for the most part, agree on the symbol and creatures that the constellation suggests. For example, Taurus is seen as a bull in both systems. Like the name *Taurus*, the Sanskrit name *Vrishabha* means *bull*. For convenience, we will use the Western names in this book, though in India, the Sanskrit names are used.

For instance, people born when the Sun was supposedly in front of the group of stars called Aries identify as an Aries Sun sign. In contrast, Vedic astrology calculates the position of all the planets at the time you were born and focuses on a rising zodiac sign. This is the constellation that appeared on the eastern horizon at the exact time, date, and location of your birth, basically showering you with blessings during your arrival into this life. So although the Sun may have been in Aries at the exact moment of your birth, on that specific day, and from that specific spot on planet Earth, Virgo may have been the constellation of stars rising on the eastern horizon, making you a Virgo rather than an Aries.

This attachment to Western Sun signs was exemplified by my youngest sister, who, despite our identical upbringing, happily identifies with her Western zodiac sign. "*Dada* (brother), it's like a sports team. If you grew up in Chicago, and you support the Bears, no matter where you move later in life, you will always be a Bears fan, even if they keep losing. Your zodiac sign is like the sports team you identify with; don't tell me after all this time that I have to switch teams!"

In my sister's case, her Western zodiac (Sun) sign is Leo, but by Vedic calculations, she's a Scorpio, because that was the constellation rising on the eastern horizon when she was born. This more personalized calculation of your birth sign yields a much deeper, soul-level picture of you, perhaps even a hidden personality covered by years of ego construction, which some people aren't ready for—even modern-day Western yogis.

The Vedic Knowledge System

Ancient India developed a massive system of human self-improvement that contains enough knowledge to fill several floors of a library. From this Vedic knowledge framework emerged the widely known system of yoga. Though typically practiced as a stretching and fitness routine, yoga has been proven to cultivate greater well-being. As we explore the broader system behind yoga, we find a natural integration with Vedic astrology, its sister approach to well-being.

Let's start on the mat and move up; yoga as a postural stretching exercise is but one aspect of an eight-part integrated system known as the eight limbs of yoga, or *ashtanga* in Sanskrit (see Fig. 1). The first limb (*yamas*) gives guidelines on personal behaviors; the second (*niyamas*), guidelines for societal conduct; the third (*asana*), the actual physical postures; and the fourth (*pranayama*), breathing and energy activation techniques. The remaining four limbs (*pratyahara, dharana, dhyana,* and *samadhi*) are various stages of meditative practice. These eight limbs form a system known as Raja Yoga, a set of techniques to connect to your deeper soul and inner wisdom. However, Raja Yoga is only one of four paths of yoga, the others being Bhakti Yoga, Karma Yoga, and Jnana Yoga—paths of devotion, service, and knowledge respectively—all equally rich and powerful paths to soul connection and inner wisdom. (Please refer to *The Business Casual Yogi* for more on the concepts of yoga.)

These four paths of yoga are just one branch of an even larger body of knowledge in the Vedic system that includes multiple disciplines of medicine, philosophy, music, mantras, rituals, pronunciation, grammar, divination, astronomy, astrology . . . and the list goes on. All of this is then topped off with an elaborate pantheon of Vedic myths and deities that leverage the power of story to expound on the teachings of those systems. You could easily spend your whole life just trying to understand one single branch.

Beyond this remarkable *intellectual* knowledge trunk, there is an adjacent trunk known as the *intuitive* knowledge trunk, and here, rather than downloading information from texts and teachings, all the knowledge of the

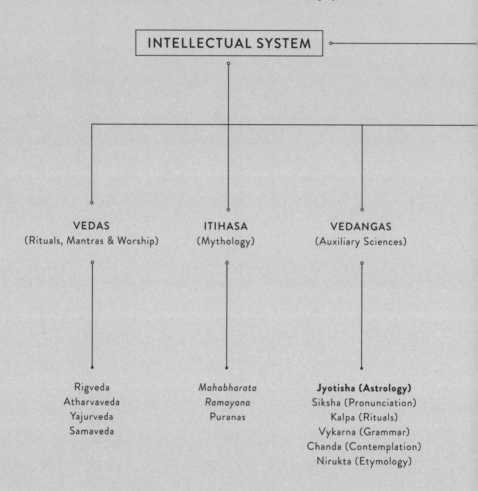

THE VEDIC KNOWLEDGE SYSTEM

NOTE: This diagram is not comprehensive. The intent is to illustrate Jyotisha, Ayurveda, and yoga in the context of key branches of the Vedic knowledge system.

INTELLECTUAL SYSTEM

VEDAS
(Rituals, Mantras & Worship)

ITIHASA
(Mythology)

VEDANGAS
(Auxiliary Sciences)

Rigveda
Atharvaveda
Yajurveda
Samaveda

Mahabharata
Ramayana
Puranas

Jyotisha (Astrology)
Siksha (Pronunciation)
Kalpa (Rituals)
Vykarna (Grammar)
Chanda (Contemplation)
Nirukta (Etymology)

Figure 1

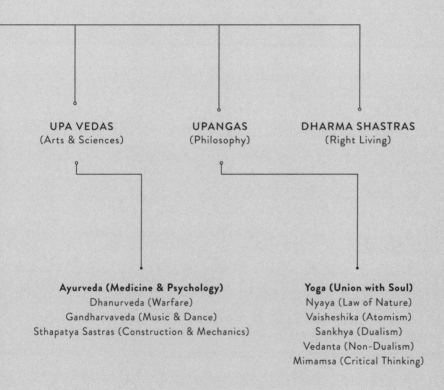

INTUITIVE SYSTEM

The intuitive system can access the entire intellectual system.

UPA VEDAS
(Arts & Sciences)

UPANGAS
(Philosophy)

DHARMA SHASTRAS
(Right Living)

Ayurveda (Medicine & Psychology)
Dhanurveda (Warfare)
Gandharvaveda (Music & Dance)
Sthapatya Sastras (Construction & Mechanics)

Yoga (Union with Soul)
Nyaya (Law of Nature)
Vaisheshika (Atomism)
Sankhya (Dualism)
Vedanta (Non-Dualism)
Mimamsa (Critical Thinking)

Deep knowledge in any one branch offers insight into other branches.

Vedic system is supposedly available to us through the deep recesses of our own intuition. Perhaps this is why so much of the system makes sense to us when we start to become practitioners of any one branch.

As validation of the power of human intuition, the entire Vedic knowledge system was cognized by the ancient sages of India known as the *rishis*. These enlightened seers lived fifteen thousand years ago along the banks of the Indus River, at the base of the mighty Himalayas. Men and women of this Indus River Valley civilization sat in deep states of meditation for hours on end, for generations and millennia, each going deep into their own consciousness and discovering and perfecting a system of universal consciousness for humanity. These insights were debated, collated, and codified into an oral tradition where knowledge was passed down from parent to child to grandchild in poetic verses numbering in the tens of thousands. About five thousand years ago, these teachings were finally written down in a series of texts known as the Vedas. Though numerous world cultures have developed systems of human self-development and spirituality, none are as ancient, as comprehensive, or as integrated as the Vedic knowledge system. It is from this elegant body of knowledge that Vedic astrology emerged.

The Three Layers of Consciousness

A fundamental tenet of the Vedic knowledge system is that we have three layers of consciousness to our being, which are often referred to in the West as the body, mind, and soul. These everyday terms derive from the Sanskrit *sthula sharira*, *sukshma sharira*, and *karana sharira*, which mean *physical body*, *subtle body*, and *causal body*, respectively.

Our physical body consists of our physical anatomy, which includes our bones, muscles, joints, and organs. The animation of our being comes from the subtle body, or energetic layer, which has its parallel system of subtle anatomy through which the *prana* life-force energy flows (referred to as *chi* in East Asian traditions). This is also the layer in which our emotions, thinking, intellect, and sense of ego reside. The deeper, more profound

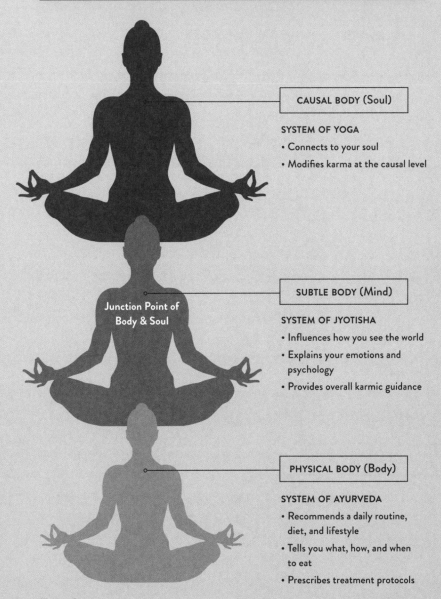

LAYERS OF HUMAN CONSCIOUSNESS

CAUSAL BODY (Soul)

SYSTEM OF YOGA
- Connects to your soul
- Modifies karma at the causal level

SUBTLE BODY (Mind)

SYSTEM OF JYOTISHA
- Influences how you see the world
- Explains your emotions and psychology
- Provides overall karmic guidance

Junction Point of Body & Soul

PHYSICAL BODY (Body)

SYSTEM OF AYURVEDA
- Recommends a daily routine, diet, and lifestyle
- Tells you what, how, and when to eat
- Prescribes treatment protocols

Figure 2

layer is our causal body, which is often referred to as our soul, our deeper consciousness or higher self, as described in the modern literature around spiritual intelligence. This soul layer is often accessed by practitioners of spiritual and religious traditions, a layer through which we connect to our innate divine intelligence. The Vedic knowledge system correlates each of these layers of being to specific systems of personal development that help align, integrate, and activate these integral parts of our being, enabling smoother sailing through life (see Fig. 2).

Focused on the physical body, the system of Ayurveda, the mind-body medicine system of the Vedic tradition, helps us identify our unique psycho-somatic disposition to favor the right lifestyle, diet, herbs, exercise, and medical interventions to balance our physical well-being and heal us from disease. At the deepest soul level, the systems of yoga help us to connect to our deeper nature and innate spiritual intelligence.

The mind serves as a junction point that connects the soul and body layers. Within this coupling layer, we create and experience the ups and downs of life and interpret our very existence and sense of self. It is from the mind layer that we make choices, experience emotions, and exercise our will to shape what we can in our physical world. From the mind, we experience and influence our very destiny by making our choices and decisions. Vedic astrology is the sophisticated system that targets this junction point of body, mind, and soul and helps us deeply understand our human manifestation to better navigate life's journey.

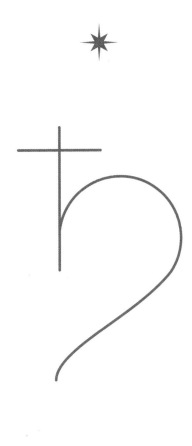

CHAPTER 2
Karma and Vedic Astrology

Vedic astrology is known as Jyotish in Sanskrit and is composed of two root words: *jyotir* (light) and *isha* (soul consciousness, divine consciousness, or inner consciousness). Jyotish therefore is the study of the light of our consciousness. It addresses the layer of our being where karma resides. Karma is a fundamental pillar of the Vedic knowledge system that teaches that every action you take will have some consequence and that current consequences are a result of past actions. In pop-culture terms, "What goes around comes around." In science, this correlates to Newton's third law of motion, which states that "every action must have an equal and opposite reaction," a fundamental underpinning of our physical universe. The Vedic system takes this concept further, into the subtle and causal universe—in other words, into the realm of consciousness. Karma teaches that every action you take in your life is accounted for and eventually gets paid back. This was humorously illustrated in the TV series *The Good Place*, where Ted Danson shows recently deceased souls entering the Good Place an electronic balance sheet of every deed they have ever done during their life—good ones in green and bad ones in red—to determine what happens next. In Vedic mythology, the celestial accountant is Chitragupta, who greets you at the pearly gates with a file in hand containing your karmic balance sheet and, based on this, determines where you go next.

The Vedic purpose of life, therefore, is to balance out your karmic debts by making good choices and taking good actions aligned with your soul. Any bad actions or misaligned choices add to your debt, while good actions and soul-aligned choices improve your karmic credits. All of the spiritual texts and practices of the Vedic tradition center on approaches to improve your karma. Vedic astrology specifically centers on understanding what that karma is and less-painful ways to pay off its balance. Every circumstance you face in life can be an opportunity to pay back karmic debts in a more pleasant way. As an analogy, when you finish a meal at a restaurant, there are many ways to pay for this meal. Cash, check, credit card, washing dishes, or getting arrested for theft if you dine and dash. I prefer the credit card myself. But of course then I must pay the bill when it eventually comes in the mail, or else there will be a hit to my credit score. The rub, though, is that you must be aware that you had the meal. In the case of long-forgotten meals from previous lifetimes, a Vedic astrologer is able to identify and recommend simpler ways to pay back those past debts that are coming due in this life. Karma is essentially actions and choices (across lifetimes) that eventually precipitate circumstances (in a specific lifetime), which then provide the opportunity for further choices and actions. You thus have ultimate choice—and ultimate responsibility—to manage your karma and its consequences.

Karma and Vedic astrology are inextricably linked, because Vedic astrology is fundamentally an analysis of our individual karma coupled with a system of tools to manage it. The system teaches that every soul has a closet full of karma that they are burdened with after many, many choices and actions, over many, many lifetimes. However, in this single lifetime, we only bring a carry-on bag of karma to work through—just enough that we can still fit it in the overhead bin. We are given multiple lifetimes to work out all our karma, like a karmic-debt payment plan, otherwise it would be too overwhelming. Some hardy souls, however, must pay off multiple karmic debts in one lifetime. If you face many challenges in life, given that your soul takes on only what it can handle, you can find comfort in the fact that you are likely an evolved soul.

The Vedic astrologer casts a diagram (horoscope) of the sky at the moment a human takes their first breath. This diagram of the planets and stars in space is said to be a reflection of the soul that has attached to that budding body and mind, incarnated into human form. By analyzing this birth chart, the Vedic astrologer assesses that one carry-on bag of karma that the person will bear though life and determines when various items from that bag will be pulled out, because it doesn't all happen at once. Jyotish is designed to help you understand what events will arise and when, and how they will influence your personality, your appearance, your mind, your environment, your choices, your relationships, and the consequences you will face (good and bad) due to that carry-on bag of karma.

This then brings us back to yoga, one of the most potent remedial measures connected to Jyotish. Yoga consists of practices that take us beyond the subtle body into the realm of the causal body, or deeper soul consciousness. Through yoga, we can address and balance karma at the root level and make more soul-aligned choices. As many serious yogis will tell you, their life, mindset, physical being, relationships, choices, and consciousness shift through their yogic practices.

These three systems—Ayurveda, Jyotish, and yoga—elegantly integrate to tackle the three key layers of our being and are like the three legs of a stool that support who we are. In ancient times, this integration was well understood; however, with our modern penchant for compartmentalizing knowledge into discrete boxes, we've lost sense of that integration. Yoga has been reduced to a stretching exercise. Ayurveda is just emerging and lacks the credibility of extensive research and sophisticated marketing that Western medicine enjoys. Jyotish is barely known in modern Western culture, dismissed in favor of its Western counterpart. But just as you might contrast gymnastics and yoga (physical stretching versus an integrated mind-body-soul karma-balancing practice), you could contrast Western astrology, a casual, pop-culture psychology system, with Jyotish, an integrated mind-body-soul understanding of your life.

Differences between Western Astrology and Jyotish

REALITY-BASED CALCULATIONS

With the understanding of the immense ecosystem that is the backdrop for Vedic astrology, we can see how orphaned and simplistic mainstream Western astrology might appear to a practitioner of Jyotish. A basic challenge in Western astrology, especially for my skeptical engineering mind, is that the calculations for planetary positions aren't based in reality. When you look up the Western zodiac sign of your birth, it's supposed to indicate the location of the Sun during that month against the backdrop of the zodiac constellations surrounding Earth; however, the Sun wasn't actually in that location, astronomically speaking. In other words, the Western zodiac Sun sign is incorrect in reference to actual space. In contrast, Vedic astrology relies on accurate astronomy to locate the planet's positions at the time of birth, including the Sun. As I learned from an astronomer friend, modern astronomy would disagree with Western astrological calculations, yet it would agree with a Vedic astrologer on planetary and zodiac positions.

It appears that about two thousand years ago, the Vedic calculations and the Western calculations aligned. Vedic astrology, for more than five thousand years, has relied on a specific fixed star in space (Chitra, known as Spica in Western astronomy) to determine the starting point of the first zodiac sign of Aries. This same spot is where the Western zodiac started as well, two thousand years ago. (I hypothesize that this may be when the Western system was developed, possibly using the Vedic system as a starting point, because the newer Western system shares so many elements with the older Vedic system, such as zodiac sign symbolism and interpretation.) However, instead of mapping to the fixed star that Vedic astrologers had used for millennia, the Western astrologers noted the location of sunrise on the day of the spring equinox to calculate the start of the first sign of the zodiac. Due to the way the Earth rotates on its axis (with a slight wobble), that equinox point shifts every year. So now, two thousand years later, that point has shifted almost 24 degrees from the original point (within the 360-degree circle of sky surrounding Earth).

What used to be the beginning of Aries for a Western astrologer has now shifted backward to the sign before Aries, which is Pisces. You may have heard references to the Age of Aquarius, which celebrates the Western zodiac shifting back even further from reality, into the previous sign of Aquarius. Basically, the start of the Western zodiac (Aries) will continue to drift backward each year, until that purported Aries point starts in the actual constellation of Aquarius (around the year 2600.) This constructed view of the sky correlates to the concept of your constructed ego at a snapshot in time, rather than a view into the true, enduring reality of your soul. (There are some Western astrologers who have recently started to use Vedic calculations to develop a more accurate birth chart, calling it a *sidereal* calculation, which means calculations based on fixed stars.)

RISING SIGN VERSUS SUN SIGN

While Western astrology focuses on where the Sun was when you were born (though an incorrect location), Vedic astrology focuses on a point in space called the rising sign or ascendant sign, or *lagna* in Sanskrit, meaning *attached to*. The Western Sun sign implies that everyone in a thirty-day period has the same sign that they identify with (and root for), regardless of where they were born or what year. In contrast, the rising sign (accurately calculated) refers to the point on the eastern horizon that was rising into view at the moment of your birth, on the day of your birth, during that year, at the exact geographical location where you were born. This then becomes the starting point of a zodiac chart specific to you. The constellation that is the backdrop to this ascending point on the horizon can vary within hours of your birth, because the eastern horizon is constantly changing (analogous to the Sun rising in the east, and then moving through the sky as the day progresses). The eastern horizon point is also different depending on where you are on Earth (analogous to sunrise happening at different times at different locations on Earth). This specificity of birth date, birth year, birth time, and birth location, reinforced with accurate astronomical math, is a requirement to cast a Vedic birth chart that is much more specific to you and your soul journey. For instance, Albert Einstein has a Western-calculated Pisces Sun sign, which would suggest a spiritual and mystical disposition as his key personality trait, while his Vedic rising sign is Gemini, which would make intelligence and rational thought his key personality trait.

SYSTEM OF REMEDIAL MEASURES

Because Vedic astrology is a study of your unique karmic blueprint, rather than a superficial analysis of your psychology, it takes a karmic view of everything. From the vast backdrop of the Vedic knowledge system, there is a correspondingly vast system of remedial karmic measures to balance challenging energies indicated in your birth chart. These remedies are drawn from various branches of the Vedic system, including Ayurveda, yoga, music, mantras, chants, rituals, worship practices, fire rituals, mythology, gemstones, lifestyle changes, charity, and service work. Western astrology, while it may help you understand your constructed ego, does not include the concept of karma, and so it offers limited remedial measures to attenuate energies and karmas within a chart. For instance, in my practice, a client struggling with confidence can be given a yoga sequence to improve their Sun energy (planet of self-confidence), and soon they start to have more confidence through that energetic remedy. They could also take specific herbs, practice specific mantras, or wear a particular gemstone, all related to improving their Sun energy, for a similar effect.

A LIVING SPIRITUAL TRADITION

The Vedic system of astrology is in regular use by over one billion Indians across the globe, and has been used in India for over five thousand years. To this day, Jyotish is used for choosing dates and times for auspicious occasions, such as when to have a wedding ceremony (in addition to evaluating partner compatibility), start a job, make an investment, celebrate festivals, begin construction, or have a medical procedure—in other words, optimizing the birth chart of the important event for a better outcome.

Vedic astrology also has a powerful predictive ability based on which planets are in more intense energy states during different times of life (based on your unique birth timing) and where planets are currently located in space (based on their actual position), relative to your birth chart. The predictions, as I outlined in my own case, can be uncanny but helpful. A good astrologer can help you understand the planetary weather forecast so that you can better prepare yourself and avoid getting totally drenched with your karma. A relatable analogy might be that you want to do some construction, but by paying attention to the weather forecast, you adjust the construction schedule to avoid rain, or plan on appropriate equipment to mitigate the challenge. An astrologer similarly uses the energetic forecast in your life to help you plan for anything from investments to marriage to job changes to divorce settlements to asking for a raise . . . and of course when to start construction.

MULTIPLE BRANCHES AND USES

Jyotish itself is a complex system with many sub-branches, all in service of understanding our deeper nature (see Fig. 3). Ancillary systems, such as palmistry, face reading, omenology (study of omens), numerology, and other divination tools are mostly forgotten. Some branches are still well practiced, such as medical astrology, which can be used to understand the nature and timing of disease, preventative measures, and treatment protocols. I have witnessed the power of medical astrology when clients with mysterious diseases have asked for Jyotish help to determine the root cause of their health challenges. Through a simple birth chart analysis, I have been able to suggest the specific organ systems to focus on, helping the doctor to better target their diagnostics. Even weighing decisions between surgical intervention versus drug protocols versus natural treatment approaches (or karmic-balancing approaches) can be supported through Jyotish.

Jyotish can help us better plan our lives, tune in to the natural flow of the universe, and live in a more soul-aligned way. It can also be used to assess soul-level compatibility between romantic partners and business partners as well as inform better ways to interact with your karmically connected relationships, such as your family members and coworkers. In the following chapters,

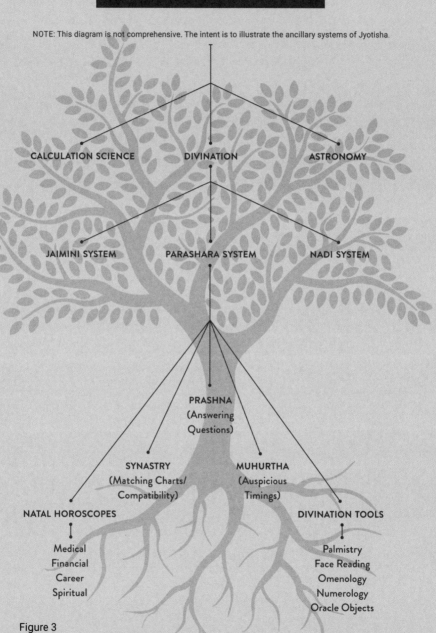

THE BRANCHES OF JYOTISHA

NOTE: This diagram is not comprehensive. The intent is to illustrate the ancillary systems of Jyotisha.

CALCULATION SCIENCE   DIVINATION   ASTRONOMY

JAIMINI SYSTEM   PARASHARA SYSTEM   NADI SYSTEM

PRASHNA
(Answering
Questions)

SYNASTRY
(Matching Charts/
Compatibility)

MUHURTHA
(Auspicious
Timings)

NATAL HOROSCOPES

Medical
Financial
Career
Spiritual

DIVINATION TOOLS

Palmistry
Face Reading
Omenology
Numerology
Oracle Objects

Figure 3

we will focus on leveraging this system to understand and better manage your unique personality and how to better understand other personalities.

As K. N. Rao, a prolific *jyotishi* (Vedic astrologer) once said:

> Jyotish is not meant to make you a fatalist but asks you to become intelligently spiritual. It is the link between ordinary reality and the highest reality. It reminds you that there is a much greater cosmic force about which you may have been negligent. It teaches you to live beautifully.

CHAPTER 3

The Nine Planets of the Celestial Court

Our entire universe depends on the rhythmic patterns of various celestial bodies. Within our solar system, the movement of the Earth around the Sun sets a specific rhythm that continuously affects our lives. Though the Sun is fixed in space, from our perspective on Earth, the Sun appears to move around us. We interpret that perceived motion and determine our daily and seasonal cycles, including daylight, nightfall, summer, and winter. The daily cycle affects our hormones and moods, creating the circadian rhythm that enables us to wake up and be alert or wind down and drift off to sleep. The seasonal cycles determine our climate, our seasonal temperature swings from winter to summer, as well as the cycles of energy that grow our food for our physical existence. Plants, through their absorption of sunlight, become our source of energy (and that of the animals that are raised for food). The Sun is our ultimate source of energy.

On a more mental level, the cycles of the Moon, as it orbits the Earth, create another set of rhythms as it waxes and wanes and moves through the sky. This lunar cycle affects bodies of water, from tides in the ocean to our own bodies, which are approximately 55 to 65 percent water As any emergency-room doctor or police officer will tell you, they see a spike of incidents during the full Moon, and even labor and delivery physicians see a similar spike of births.

Beyond the obvious solar and lunar influences on our lives, the influence of more distant celestial bodies is not as apparent. The rhythmic movement of planets such as Mercury, Venus, or Mars relative to Earth is not as well understood, but these celestial bodies *do* have an effect. As they rotate around the Sun, from Earth's perspective they move through the sky, which creates other cycles that influence us. Sometimes, from Earth's perspective, planets appear to move backward through the sky, creating the much talked-about retrograde phenomenon. For instance, when a planet like Mercury goes retrograde, many people experience technology and communication challenges.

Vedic astrology is the study of the planets and how they affect our earthly existence and rhythms. Though these massive gravitational objects may seem nothing more than a collection of rocks and gases, on a subtle level, they have powerful influences. As described previously, we consist of a physical, subtle, and causal layer of being. The Vedic knowledge system understands that the planets have similar corresponding layers—a physical layer (the rocks and gases), as well as subtle and causal layers that affect us at those corresponding levels. In Vedic astrology, the planets are said to be agents of karma, and so whatever we are due to face in life, the planets deliver to us via our subtle and causal bodies. Our personalities, mindsets, and various events in our lives are said to be under the management of the planets. If we are conscious of their influence, we can temper what they deliver to us and even influence how their effects are delivered. Studying these planets can help us understand why we are the way we are, and why we have the lives and relationships that we do.

Vedic astrology understands the karmic influence of planets, but only through those that we can see with our naked eye, without the aid of optical equipment such as telescopes. If we can see the planet, it can "see" and influence us at our karmic level. Vedic astrology is centered on the two luminaries, the Sun and the Moon (regarded as planets), as well as Mercury, Venus, Mars, Jupiter, and Saturn, the farthest planet we can see without the aid of a telescope. Uranus, Neptune, and Pluto are not a part of traditional Vedic astrology. This gives us seven of the planets used in Vedic astrology, along with two shadow planets, known as Rahu and Ketu, which are not really planets but points in space where lunar or solar eclipses occur. In Western astrology, these are called lunar nodes. When we add in these two nodes, we arrive at the complete list of nine planets used in Vedic astrology.

The Sanskrit word for planet is *graha*, which means *to seize or grasp*. In Vedic astrology, it's useful to think of the planets being able to karmically grasp us at a subtle level, causing us to take various actions or face various consequences. This concept of grasping also clarifies why a star such as the Sun, or Earth's satellite, the Moon, are considered grahas. Their consciousness-grasping quality is not captured in the translated word *planet*, though this is a convenient word for a Western audience. The *navagraha*, or nine grahas—the Sun, the Moon, Mars, Mercury, Jupiter, Venus, Saturn, Rahu, and Ketu—each have certain personalities and attributes, which are easily recognized in the behaviors we engage in and see around us. Their Sanskrit names also have powerful meanings and have been used as mantras and in worship for millennia: respectively, Surya, Chandra, Mangala, Budha, Guru, Shukra, Shani, Rahu, and Ketu. Beyond the physical layers of rock and gas, these planets have a subtle and causal layer with rich personalities, through which we can better understand and interact with them.

Without needing to analyze a birth chart, we can learn to observe personalities, behaviors, and events around us and link them to how the various planets are manifesting in our life experience. We can think of each planet as representing a specific archetype, and by understanding that archetype, we can understand and even predict how certain people behave and respond to the world around them. Think of each planet as a grouping of energies. When you witness personalities or events that are similar to a planet's archetypal energy, you can be more aware of the type of energy that is at play and take steps to balance that energy as needed, via your understanding of the planets. Our life events can also help us to understand which planetary energies may be out of balance.

We will get to know each of these planets from both an archetypal energy point of view and from a personality point of view, leveraging the richness of Vedic mythology, the vehicle through which the Vedic knowledge system has been shared throughout the ages. The ancients understood that not every deep spiritual concept can be reduced to mere words and logic, but rather that they need to be energetically understood and absorbed across the layers of our being beyond the mind. This energetic wisdom is imparted through story. Though in English the word *mythology* suggests a myth or false belief, in the Vedic system, these are living patterns of energy that exist throughout time. As we begin to understand these stories, we start to connect with the energies underlying them and discover a connection in ourselves to the very essence of universal energies that have pervaded time. Through mythology, we start to activate ourselves beyond just our intellect and mental faculties and can tap into our rich intuitive abilities (which the ancients described as residing in our subtle bodies). So though the stories may not always make logical sense, notice your intuitive connection to the patterns described in them and how those patterns might relate to your life circumstances and relationships.

Many of these stories are thousands of years old, with their original texts lost to time. Each tale is rich and complex, with the potential to fill an entire book. I have attempted to capture the key energetic narrative through my own condensed and simplified retelling of the stories. If you feel drawn to a deeper study of Vedic mythology, you can explore some of the resources in the bibliography. However, note that based on the consciousnesses of different teachers and writers, these stories can shift in detail from one retelling to another. As you absorb the stories, consider the mythological characters as manifestations and archetypes of planetary energies, without getting lost in incongruent details.

The Planetary Order

The Vedic order of the planets always begins with the Sun, the graha around which everything orbits (including our own lives), followed by the Moon, the closest graha to Earth, which is illuminated by the Sun. Then we follow with Mars, Mercury, Jupiter, Venus, Saturn, and finally the two shadow planets,

Rahu and Ketu. One way to remember this planetary order is to think about the planets and their statuses as part of a royal court. The Sun is thought of as the king of the planets, possessing bold and powerful energy, while the Moon, a reflective and nurturing energy, is the queen. Following these two royal figures is Mars, the commander in chief, who ensures the defense of the royal court. Next is Mercury, who is seen as the royal prince, in line for the throne. Then comes Jupiter, who is the senior advisor to the royal family. The next advisor is Venus, the diplomat who strategizes to keep peace with other kingdoms. Finally, Saturn, the head of the servants of the court, is the seventh planet in the lineup. Rahu and Ketu, eccentric and living in the shadows, are seen as outcastes of the court. Rahu is the innovator who does things differently, breaking all the rules of the land but bringing about change in the kingdom. Ketu is more of a recluse and renunciate, who does not want to participate in the society of the kingdom, preferring to live the life of an ascetic.

This order is also reflected in the days of the week. The ancient rishis sensed daily shifts in energy, recurring every seven days, correlating to each of the visible grahas. Sunday was the day when the Sun was traditionally felt and worshipped in ancient times, and so it was given the name Ravivar, Ravi being one of the names of the Sun, and var meaning lord of the day. Monday is the day of the Moon's influence, and was given the name Somvar, Soma being one of the names of the Moon. This connection was retained with the modern English Monday, as well as being reflected in the French and Spanish words for the Moon, Lundi and Lunes (derived from the Latin name for the Moon, Luna). Tuesday was connected to Mars energy and given the name Mangalvar. In French and Spanish, Mardi and Martes preserve the original planetary reference, while the English word Tuesday refers to the Norse god of war, Tiw. Wednesday is connected to Budhvar, or Mercury energy, as you can see in French (Mercredi) and Spanish (Miércoles). The English Wednesday comes from the Norse god Woden, who's equated with the Roman god Mercury. Thursday, or Thor's day, is also Guruvar, Jupiter's day (Jeudi and Jueves in French and Spanish). Friday, Shukravar, is ruled by Venus (Vendredi and Viernes in French and Spanish). The word Friday comes from Frigg, the Norse goddess of fertility (a trait also connected to Venus). The last planet is Saturn, which provides the name for Shanivar, and is where we get the English word Saturday.

In India to this day, people wishing to receive grace from a certain planet will perform rituals to propitiate that planet on its specific day of the week. While growing up, I remember my father avoiding travel on Tuesdays and Saturdays (Mars and Saturn, respectively), because those two planets could create challenges. These days, I notice that Tuesdays and Saturdays happen to be the slowest travel days at the airport (days on which I have also often availed myself of cheaper airfare). If you are an advanced student of yoga or a person sensitive to energies, you may well notice the different qualities of each planet reflected within each day of the week and be able to leverage them as needed. This explains why Saturday is traditionally avoided as a day for marriage in India, because Saturn relates to separation and challenges. Our high divorce rates in the West may have some correlation to Saturday being the most popular day for Western weddings. (Friday, being Venus's day, a planet of love and harmony, is a better choice.)

To understand the individual personified characteristics of each planet, we will share a mix of traditional Vedic teaching tales and the typical attributes associated with each planet. As you read about each planet, think of themes and events in your life related to those energies, and of people and relationships in your life that remind you of each planet's archetype. You won't have a birth chart for every person and situation you encounter; however, when you learn about the unique personality signature of each planet, you will notice their archetypal energy showing up in every facet of your life. For instance, as you learn about the violent nature of Mars, when you encounter an aggressive person, you can easily relate their behavior to an excess of Mars energy. Also note that there are many stories related to each planet. They may switch gender and even personality depending on the focus of a particular story. A good student of astrology can keep multiple conflicting concepts in mind simultaneously to catalyze meaning at an energetic level.

In this book we will study the nine planets of the Vedic system, which correspond to not only the nine digits of our numbering system but also the seven days of the week (the seven visible planets). They are also usually presented in the order of the days of the week: Sun (Surya), Moon (Chandra), Mars (Mangala), Mercury (Budha), Jupiter (Guru), Venus (Shukra), and Saturn (Shani), followed by the two shadow planets, Rahu and Ketu.

CHAPTER 4

Sun and Moon: The King and the Queen

Sun (Surya) ☉

The Sun is the king of the grahas, and it is the luminary that provides light to the other planets. All planets revolve around the Sun. You could say that people that embody Sun energy are naturally bright, radiant, and bold personalities who attract people to follow them and tend to have an orbit of people around them. Because the Sun is also the planet responsible for providing the energy for our existence, people who have a lot of Sun energy are natural leaders who energize others and may have a lot of people dependent on them. As the Sun, they are powerhouses of energy and vitality, often having strong immune systems. They can embody strong creative abilities, creating new life through different endeavors and ideas. They also have strong senses of pride and achievement.

In Vedic mythology, the Sun is known as Surya and was born to a sage named Kashyapa and his wife Aditi. (In mantras, such as the opening mantra of this book, the Sun is often referred to as Aditya, which translates to *son of Aditi*. Surya was married to Samjna, and together they had three children. But Surya (being a personification of the Sun) gave off so much heat that Samjna couldn't physically handle it anymore. She came up with a plan to take a break from him for a little while. Using her magical powers, she imbued her shadow with life force and named this shadow Chaya (which means *shadow* in Sanskrit). Samjna then left Surya's palace, leaving Chaya in her place, instructing her to act as Surya's wife but under no circumstances allowing Surya to make love to her. Surya, in all his brightness, did not even notice that his real wife had left, and he happily enjoyed the company of Chaya. One day, while feeling especially amorous, Surya made love to Chaya. Chaya ignored the warning she had been given—and continued to do so—eventually giving birth to three children, one of whom was Shani (the personification of the planet Saturn). Over time, it became obvious that Chaya favored her own children over Samjna's children (as in many a stepmother tale), even going so far as to insult Samjna's children. Surya noticed this behavior and discovered that he had been deceived. He begged for Samjna to return, which she agreed to on the condition that he reduce the intensity of his heat. To do so, Surya would have to go to the celestial architect, Vishvakarma. Using his divine milling and cutting machines, Vishvakarma chiseled away some of the radiance of the Sun to reduce his intensity. The removed parts became powerful weaponry gifted to various gods (such as Shiva's trident, Vishnu's discus, and Kartikeya's spear). Samjna was pleased with this cooling makeover and returned home, reuniting with Surya and reabsorbing Chaya (her shadow) into her being.

This tale reveals many qualities of the Sun's personality, such as a tendency to be too hot, to not see things clearly, to be cheerfully ignorant (especially with people in their immediate orbit), and to have challenges with family and children. People with Sun personalities are kinglike in their nature and enjoy being the center of attention. They shine brightly, which works well in society at large but can be overpowering at home. If a Sun personality is adequately shaped (chiseled), then the heat can become tolerable. They are naturally loving and kind, and therefore will go to the effort to make things right at home. Extreme Sun types experience many challenges in their relationships and need to cool it in order for things to work out. They also like to follow a routine—rising with the sun and winding down as it gets dark, in line with circadian rhythms. They work very well with institutions and hierarchies and have a keen understanding of the order of things. With this comes an innate understanding of hierarchy and how to manage and influence various power structures and systems to exert their will. They make great politicians and corporate leaders. They are usually also very strong-willed and have powerful principles and ideals. They may find it difficult to work for other people, being so kingly in nature. They often resort to starting their own business (or kingdom).

QUALITIES OF A STRONG SUN TYPE

- Is a natural leader with confidence, a strong character, and a bold and assertive nature.

- Shows up as a bright, shining, dignified, and energizing personality.

- Is authoritative, but can be harsh (burning other people).

- Likes to be the center of attention and in charge. Can make people become dependent on them.

- Is kind, generous, and willing to work to change themselves.

- Can see the big picture clearly, but can miss the details.

- Stands up for the truth and what is right. Has high ideals.

- Can have a sense of invincibility.

- Is good at getting people to bend to their will. Good at politics and managing hierarchies.

- Likes to follow a regular rhythm (especially aligned with the Sun).

- Is often very creative and can launch new ideas and ventures into the world.

- Likes to wear bright and colorful clothing, especially yellow, gold, and orange hues (colors associated with Sun energy).

Moon (Chandra) ☽

In the same way that the Sun is the king of the planetary court, the Moon is the queen. She is also a powerful ruler, but she is more connected to the emotions and moods of the court and the people. Though the Moon is its own planet, it receives and reflects its light from the Sun, so people who have strong Moon energy have a reflective quality about them, and also have a kind of luminosity to their appearance. They feed on the energy of other people, both of their close circle and of the masses. Moon-oriented people can be very sensitive to the news of the world, and their moods can fluctuate depending on the overall energy of the world around them. This also gives them a quality of being very aware of the moods of the masses, which means they can make very good politicians (who in essence reflect the light of their constituents, good or bad).

Just as the Moon waxes and wanes, the moods of Moon types shift. Due to their queen energy, they are usually very nurturing and patient and have powerful emotional intelligence. A Moon type can have very strong emotions, both in their expression of love for others and in their anger if they are disturbed. They also have deep intuition and perception to truly understand what is going on beneath the surface of a person or situation. They can read a room easily and deftly. They have a keen ability to both sense and settle the energy of others, because they tend to have an overall calm demeanor. When a Sun type enters a room, regardless of how the room is feeling, that person exerts their energy (even if it makes others uncomfortable). In contrast, a Moon type senses the room and adjusts themselves to create synergy and comfort. As the queen, the Moon is responsible for hosting at the court and providing good hospitality. Similarly, Moon types love to host at their homes and ensure that others are comfortable and taken care of.

The Moon, with all this heart energy and emotion, is a hopeless romantic, constantly lusting after others. Given that the Moon waxes and wanes, it is not only moody but flits from one romantic interest to another. In one tale, Chandra (the Moon as a handsome young man) was a student of Brihaspati, a personification of Jupiter. Brihaspati had a wisdom school, where his wife, Tara, cooked and attended to the students. Chandra started to lust after Tara, his teacher's wife. Tara was feeling ignored by Brihaspati, who was absorbed in his rituals. And so Chandra, with his luminous radiance and loving nature, caught the attention of Tara. Chandra showered Tara with attention and affection, and she was smitten. Together, they escaped to Chandra's lovely and comfortable palace away from the more austere school environment of Brihaspati. After some time, they had a son together, Budha (the personification of Mercury and seen as the rational mind, in contrast to the emotional mind of his father, Chandra) This illegitimate child was a major scandal, made even worse when Chandra—with his fickle nature—moved on to his next romantic interest and Tara was left with a son and no partner.

From this tale, we understand the hopeless romantic nature of Moon types and the powerful emotional energies that cause them to do things beyond the norms of society, which can leave lasting consequences. We also see in the Moon an affectionate, loving, and playful nature, but also a changeable, fickle quality, as the waxing and waning of the Moon in the sky embodies. Moon types are loveable, flirtatious, and affectionate, easily wooing and charming others as Chandra did with Tara. They also typically create very comfortable homes that become like their own private palaces.

The Moon is connected to all matters of the heart, and particularly the emotional and nurturing heart, which is often connected with mothering energy. The Moon is a divine mother as consort to the Sun, the divine father. These mothering qualities show up in people in the way they relate to others—as a partner, as a boss, as a friend—regardless of their gender or their parental status. They also have amazing qualities of intuition and like to interact with people from a heart-centered place. With all this emotional energy, they are the first to tear up during a touching moment.

QUALITIES OF A STRONG MOON TYPE

- Is emotionally oriented. Can have powerful and changing feelings.

- Has a strong intuition and can perceive the meaning and emotions behind words.

- Is a loving, open, affectionate, and popular personality. Cares about being seen in a positive light.

- Likes to entertain others and is a natural host. Enjoys socializing.

- Can be a hopeless romantic, or constantly lusting after others.

- Is naturally friendly and likes to connect at the level of heart and meaning.

- Likes to be around people; does not usually like to be alone. Adjusts to the energy of others.

- Leads through emotional intelligence; good with managing feelings.

- Influenced by the moods of others and can be sensitive to news and the moods of the masses. Great at politics and understanding people's needs.

- Can easily bend to the will of the people.

- Drawn to water, calm, and peaceful places.

- Focuses on the person rather than the problem.

- Likes to wear white and soft, comfortable materials. Maybe even night clothing such as pajamas and sweatshirts.

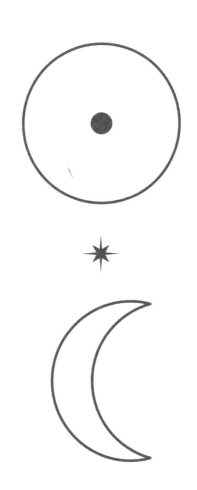

CHAPTER 5

Mars, Mercury, Jupiter, and Venus: Members of the Court

Mars (Mangala) ♂

A strong kingdom will have a strong army to defend its ideals and way of life. The general of that army is Mars, the commander in chief. Mars stands at attention, carries out orders, and gets things done. Mars types are aggressive, hard-charging, and get things done. They are willing to stand up and fight to defend their ideals (which may not always come from them, but from higher powers such as the king, the government, or corporate leadership). They are natural leaders and make excellent CEOs, executives, and commanders. As the commander in chief, Mars types have strength—not just physically but also mentally and strategically. They are very technical, constantly engineering solutions for success. Mars types are often found in uniformed services, engineering, and technical fields, as well as in high-functioning institutions and corporations. The type-A personality that I often come across in my coaching work is a Mars trait. Mars types, in their quest to get things done, can often be impatient and cruel, ignoring the feelings and emotions of others in service of the objective at hand. But those who possess too little Mars energy must focus on building courage and willpower.

In Vedic culture, Mars is represented by warrior deities—particularly Kartikeya, a god of war, who at just seven days old defeated the evil demon Taraka. As is typical with Asuras, Taraka had fallen from saintly grace into greedy, destructive, and materialistic behavior (the English translation of Asura as *demon* does not convey this subtlety). Taraka performed intense penance to further his conquering ways and was rewarded by Lord Brahma, the Creator, with the boon of being undefeatable. There was just one catch. He *could* be defeated by a seven-day-old child. Taraka, who could not imagine such a defeat by an infant, developed a sense of invincibility, let the power get to his head, and began to terrorize the world. Various gods tried to defeat him with their weaponry (fashioned from pieces of the Sun), but all were defeated by Taraka. Lord Shiva, meanwhile, ever the yogi, was disturbed from his deep meditation by all the destruction and noise. Enraged by this interruption, he produced an immense firebolt from his third eye, conceiving the baby Kartikeya. The fetus was so incredibly fiery and hot that an appropriate mother could not be found except in the cool streams of Mother Earth, which served as the womb for this child. Each day after his birth, he grew a full year in size and strength. Seven days after his birth, Kartikeya received a spear (fashioned from the Sun's spare parts), which he used to battle and eventually to destroy the demon Taraka.

With supreme confidence, Kartikeya went home to his father, Shiva, and reunited with his beloved brother Ganesh, often depicted as the elephant-headed god in Vedic lore. (Ganesh happens to be the patron deity of Vedic astrology because elephants have such amazing memory. The elephant head symbolizes going beyond the intellectual mind to access the esoteric.) Ganesh was chubby and good-natured, while muscular and fiery Kartikeya, fresh from his victory, bristled with arrogance. They challenged each other to see who could circle the world the fastest. Kartikeya, in his hastiness and zest for competition, set off at breakneck speed. Meanwhile, Ganesh, who has wisdom beyond mere intellectual intelligence, walked a calm circle around his parents, who are the world to him. Ganesh won with this brilliant tactic.

These stories illustrate the rash and arrogant nature of Mars, as well as his hotheadedness, which can only be cooled in the waters of Mother Earth. Mars types have a strong bond to the planet Earth (because Kartikeya gestated within her). Mars is sometimes called Bhomaye, which means the son of Bhoomi Ma (Bhoomi being the Earth and Ma meaning *mother*). You can also see how brawn can sometimes overpower the brain, and though Mars is highly logical, he can miss the obvious with his blustery and rash nature. Mars also can defeat seemingly impossible forces and be highly mission driven. Mars types loathe to be interrupted in their tasks or missions and tend to move and act quickly. They are extremely decisive, though they could benefit from slowing down and really understanding the path to victory, as in the case of the sibling competition between Ganesh and Kartikeya. *Act first, think later* can be a hindrance for Mars types. Mars types also tend to run quite hot and can have ruddy faces, and need to stay well hydrated to cool down. They are quick to defend causes and not easily bullied. They also have a love of competition of any kind, like sports or debate, and can be very fascinated with machines, tools, and weapons, especially if they aid in getting the job done.

QUALITIES OF A STRONG MARS TYPE

- Is rash, bold, decisive, and daring. Likes to command and be in charge.

- Has good executive and project management ability. Is good with organizing and logistics.

- Likes to get things done. Can be overly proud of accomplishments.

- Is quick thinking and quick moving. Can be impulsive.

- Is not easily bullied. Stands up for their beliefs. Is independent and resourceful.

- Is willing to argue and fight when needed (or also when *not* needed).

- Is usually strong, powerful, muscular, and athletic.

- Tends to run hot and is short-tempered.

- Can be ambitious and arrogant.

- Is task-oriented. Needs a clear mission and goal. Hates to be interrupted or have goals changed on them.

- Has passion and courage. Can be ruthless in getting things done.

- Possesses strong skills of judgment and logic, though can be overly critical and judgmental.

- Can do things to excess, especially with lifestyle choices, such as alcohol, cigarettes, meat, and fried foods.

- Likes the color red and likes to wear clothing that displays their power.

Mercury (Budha) ☿

The Sanskrit word *buddhi* means intelligence, and Mercury is fittingly the bright, intelligent, and youthful prince of the king and queen. The Sun and Moon are connected directly to masculine (solar) and feminine (lunar) energies, but Mercury's energy is more gender neutral. Though referred to as a prince, he is prepubescent, and so can take on both masculine and feminine behaviors and is in the process of exploring his identity. Being youthful, he loves to play and to act and is often found around the court mimicking others, poking fun here and there, and playacting. Because Mercury is young, he is also studying and in a phase of life of absorbing and learning knowledge and facts. These all relate to the qualities of a strong Mercury personality: playful, youthful, intelligent, and constantly thinking and learning. However, because the young royal is still immature, he can sometimes get overwhelmed with too much information and can have a hard time deciding, weighing too many facts, and getting paralysis through analysis. Mercury types can get lost in the details, lose the big picture, and be unable to make a solid decision. The youthfulness of the prince, however, makes it easy for him to adapt to and leverage technology.

As Mercury is a fast-moving planet, Mercury types are fast-moving and quick to learn new knowledge. They would be especially good at facts, trivia, and multiple languages (as a young royal would be taught at court). The young royal is also eager to make his own mark on the world and constantly trying out his different ideas through business endeavors. Mercury personalities are natural businesspeople, and are full of facts, knowledge, and intelligence. They also move around a lot, both from idea to idea and from place to place, enjoying travel and lively discussions. Mercury types excel at communication, both written and spoken, and make good orators, actors, and writers.

Mercury was born as a result of the affair between the Moon and Tara, and is the rational-mind descendant of his emotional father, the Moon. Whereas the Moon is connected to emotions and intuition, Mercury types are of a rational mind, full of logic and data-driven and fact-based thinking. Mercury types may use their logical mind more than their intuition. So as the story continues, the Moon moved on, and now Tara (Jupiter's wife) had to return home. Jupiter was very upset that his wife had left and had an affair with the Moon. Now with her returning with a young Mercury in tow, it was too stark a reminder of her transgression. Jupiter refused to take in Mercury. However, the youth was so charming and eloquent that Jupiter quickly forgave the whole thing and adopted Mercury as his own child. We can see the forgiving nature of Jupiter here but also the charming ability of Mercury. Mercury types can talk their way out of many a situation and deftly turn people to their point of view with their charm. Mercury is connected to all kinds of communication (technological or otherwise), including talking, writing, listening, and reading. Therefore, popular culture correctly associates a retrograde Mercury (traveling backward in the sky from Earth's viewpoint) with technology not working correctly and garbled communications.

QUALITIES OF A STRONG MERCURY TYPE

- Is charming, eloquent, and an excellent communicator. Can be expressive and talkative.

- Loves data, facts, information, and trivia.

- Is highly intelligent and logical.

- Sees both sides of an argument and can argue both sides. Can also be indecisive.

- Enjoys singing, dancing, and acting. Good at imitating others, and can also end up copying others in behavior and mannerisms.

- Is playful and witty. Likes to keep it light.

- Can be considered immature.

- May appear androgynous or balanced between masculine and feminine energy. Can be drawn to sexual experimentation.

- Is fast moving. Enjoys travel and exploring differing ideas.

- Is typically good with technology and communication.

- Likes the color green. Dresses youthfully and playfully.

Jupiter (Guru or Brihaspati) ♃

In the Vedic system, the planet Jupiter is bestowed with the name Guru, which means *wise teacher*, or more profoundly, *dispeller of the darkness of ignorance*. This is the planet associated with teachers, counselors, gurus, priests, and jyotishis, who all work in their respective ways to dispel the darkness of ignorance. Jupiter is the senior advisor of the court, and the king and queen consult Jupiter for all matters related to the governing of the kingdom and maintenance of the family power. Jupiter types are excellent advisors, offering counsel and wisdom. Jupiter is also responsible for overseeing all ceremonies and rituals of the court. Therefore, Jupiter types will be drawn to pomp, ceremony, and ritual.

It is this love for ritual that got Jupiter into trouble in his marriage. Recall that Brihaspati, the guru of the finest wisdom school of the universe, was married to Tara, who was yearning for her husband's attention. As she tried to seduce her husband, he waved her off, instead preferring to carry out his complex rituals, because he believed the path to a happy marriage and life was to honor tradition and devotion to God. While focused on the rituals to improve his life, he neglected to actually focus on the practical aspects of his life—devotion to his wife, Tara, whose beauty soon caught the attention of Chandra (the Moon). Tara eloped with Chandra, because he was only too ready to love and hold her. Brihaspati, absorbed in his rituals, did not at first notice Tara's departure, but when he did, he was enraged. To add insult, this wayward student, Chandra, and his wife, Tara, had a son together, Budha (Mercury). Chandra, with his fickle nature, soon tired of the relationship and parenting responsibilities, and went off to his next romantic conquest, leaving Tara with the child. She returned home, and Brihaspati, with his divine compassion and heart of forgiveness, accepted Tara back and committed to giving his wife the devotion she craved. In the ultimate act of forgiveness, charmed by the young Budha, Brihaspati adopted him as his own son. We can see the father and son partnership here. While Jupiter possesses the wisdom of the ages, Mercury has the modern, rational intelligence. Brihaspati became the guru to the gods, and is seen as the ultimate embodiment of wisdom, teaching, generosity, forgiveness, and optimism.

Jupiter types tend to be natural teachers and are sought after for their counsel and wisdom. They tend to be forgiving, empathetic, and compassionate and are drawn to traditions, ritual, and ceremony. They are usually content and have a jovial nature. They also enjoy learning, particularly ancient, traditional, spiritual, or religious knowledge. They are naturally drawn to higher education and have deep respect for formal knowledge. However, they can tend to get overly lost in ritual and tradition and stubbornly cling to their belief systems, neglecting practical considerations. An imbalanced Jupiter can give too much advice, or be too pushy with their way of thinking.

In another tale related to rituals, a relative of Jupiter, Daksha Prajapati, held a large fire-worship ceremony but decided not to invite his daughter Sati and her husband, Lord Shiva, considering him too unkempt and unruly for such an auspicious occasion. Shiva, always focusing on his yoga and meditation, usually only wearing a loincloth and covered in ashes, didn't care much for silly societal conventions and clothing norms. Daksha was also concerned about losing face, because he knew the mighty Lord Shiva would be unlikely to bow to him and touch his feet, which was the expected convention for the master of the ceremony. This exclusion annoyed Sati, who decided to show up anyway but was further insulted by her father. This drew Lord Shiva's wrath, which caused an immense turmoil in the universe. Jupiter can be associated with snobbery, elitism, exclusionary behaviors (even to one's own family), and demands of subservience, which can cause frustration and anger in others, eventually causing the downfall of a Jupiter type's empire. The tale of Nero—the hedonistic Roman emperor, lost in playing his violin while his citizens burned and his empire collapsed—is an example of a Jupiter type way out of balance. It illustrates how a Jupiter personality can become self-indulgent and out of touch with the common people.

QUALITIES OF A STRONG JUPITER TYPE

- Is drawn to education, philosophy, law, spirituality, religion, and knowledge.

- Is naturally inclined to being a teacher, advisor, and counselor.

- Has an intellectual and spiritual nature.

- Can have a heavier physique (Guru also means *heavy*).

- Can be drawn to rituals and ceremonies, but may get lost in the pomp and circumstance.

- Can be an elitist, only respecting those with status, credentials, degrees, lineage, etc.

- May be overly academic, religious, or spiritual and neglect, practical matters.

- Has an optimistic, generous, kind, benevolent, and expansive nature.

- Will sometimes demand subservience from people, or exclude certain groups and lose sight of equity and universal respect for all people. Can think their way is superior.

- Can be overly attached to convention and dogma.

- Likes the colors yellow and orange, and enjoys dressing for the occasion.

Venus (Shukra)

The Sanskrit word for Venus is Shukra and translates as *the bright one*. Sure enough, if you see Venus in the sky, it shines "bright like a diamond," as Rihanna would say. Accordingly, Venus is connected to wealth, prosperity, music, and of course, relationships and marriage, appropriately symbolized by the diamond ring used in Western culture to signal the engagement of a romantic couple. Venus types are naturally beautiful, graceful, and elegant, drawn to high design, fine art, and luxury goods. They tend to dress well, adorn themselves with jewelry and various status symbols, and enjoy the good life. Venus types enjoy music, arts, dance, and fashion. Venus-oriented people also are good at creating harmony in relationships and are constantly seeking ways for more comfort in life. In contrast to Mars, which has an energy of aggression and conquering,

Venus is more about harmony and love. In the court analogy, Venus is an advisor to the king, but whereas Jupiter focuses on more spiritual and philosophical advising, Venus is more about the everyday practical matters, seeking out diplomatic solutions to maintain peace. Venus also advises regarding the finances of the treasury and develops strategies to ensure prosperity for the kingdom. Financial advisors, investors, and art dealers would all have a healthy dose of Venus energy. Venus, like Jupiter, is also a highly learned planet, with deep wisdom and knowledge, and is a great teacher as well, however with a more inclusive approach to students than Jupiter, as seen in how he excluded his daughter and Shiva from his fire ceremony, as well as in the following story.

The story of Venus begins with the sage Angiras, who had a *gurukul*, a school that trains gurus. Brihaspati (Jupiter), his son, attended the school, along with star pupil Shukra (Venus). However, Angiras tended to favor his son for leadership roles and academic accolades. Brihaspati naturally enjoyed the attention, but Shukra became both jealous and frustrated, because he was equally intelligent and accomplished. (Though Venus is typically associated with feminine energy, in this story, Venus is personified as a man.) In rebellion, Shukra quit the school and stormed off. In protest of the strict rules of acceptance at Angiras's school, he decided to form his own school that was open to all. So it came to be that Brihaspati took over his father's school. He became the teacher of the upper classes, who had to meet strict status requirements for entry, whereas Shukra became the teacher of the people, favoring anyone with good aptitude and interest.

In Vedic lore, Brihaspati became a guru to the gods, or Devas, while Shukra became a teacher to the Asuras, which is typically translated as *demons*. The word *demon* does not quite work though, because the Asuras are themselves well educated and intelligent. They were Devas at one time but became the fallen ones, giving into temptation (lust, greed, gluttony, envy, etc.) and using their godlike spiritual powers for material gain and self-indulgence rather than spiritual evolution.

Venus became the teacher to those lost in material pursuits and sensuality. Venus types prefer to learn about investing and money-making strategies, or ways to improve their appearance or sexuality, rather than working on understanding deeper philosophy or techniques of meditation and spiritual advancement. Out-of-balance Venus types can be overly materialistic, craving the latest fashions and spending money to keep up with the latest trends. They can also indulge in sexual fantasies and pursuits, constantly chasing recognition and acknowledgment for their material conquests (remember, Venus was not properly recognized at school). Given that Venus became a teacher to the Asuras, out-of-balance Venus types may keep bad company. In a balanced form, they may be drawn to teaching, but for subjects of a more practical, real-world nature, rather than the high-flying philosophies of Jupiter. Whereas Jupiter types have a sense of privilege, heritage, tradition, and lineage, Venus types believe anyone can strive to join the ranks of the elite and privileged. Venus types are also very good musicians and artists and can lose themselves in those worlds. When oriented in a healthy way, these pursuits give them divine experiences that transcend the mind and connect to their deeper soul.

QUALITIES OF A STRONG VENUS TYPE

- Can be charming, elegant, and graceful.
- Enjoys music, arts, theater, dance, design, and culture.
- Cares about beauty, form, and aesthetics.
- Seeks harmony and balance. Is a natural diplomat.
- Enjoys luxury goods, keeping up with trends, and maintaining their appearance.
- Seeks recognition and accolades.
- Is often loving, romantic, sensual, and sexual. Is pleasure-seeking by nature.

- Values financial wealth and material success.

- Is willing to teach their ways to anyone who has sincere interest. Is willing to work with different types of people and find common ground.

- Possesses strong feminine energy. Likes to maintain harmony and good relationships.

- Likes pink, white, and pastel colors. Likes to wear fine and fashionable clothing.

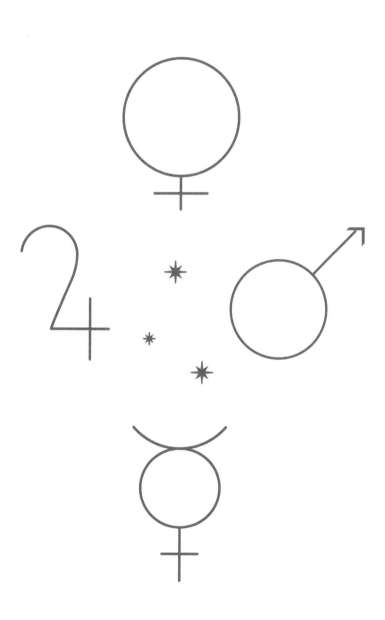

CHAPTER 6

Saturn, Rahu, and Ketu: The Servant and the Outcastes

Saturn (Shani) ♄

Saturn is the farthest planet from the Sun used in the Vedic astrology system. It is cold, lonely, and distant, in both physical and subtle attributes. Its slow orbit around the Sun earns it the name Shanaischaraya, meaning the *slow-moving one*. The word *acharya*, embedded in this name, means *teacher*, so you can think of Saturn as the slow-moving teacher, who teaches through long, drawn-out hardship, restrictions, challenges, and obstacles that lead to permanent change. In the planetary cabinet, Shani is the servant who toils away to serve the court. Saturn is connected to hard work, patience, perseverance, focus, and determination.

In the mythology of the Sun, we learned that Shani was born of Chaya, the shadow wife of the Sun, and thus Shani is seen as a shadow child of the Sun. Whereas the Sun likes to be up front and center stage, Shani resents his father's excessive brightness and prefers to stay in the background— out of sight, avoiding the limelight. It is said the gaze of Shani can cause grave misfortune, contributing to him staying in the shadows. He is resentful of his father for reuniting with his stepmother, Samjna, causing his own mother, Chaya, to once again become a shadow.

In the case of baby Ganesh's birth, all the gods were invited to give their blessing. Parvati, his mother, insisted Shani come as well, despite Shani's warning that wherever he goes, he causes misfortune. (He had previously crippled his father's charioteer with his gaze.) When he did arrive, he kept his gaze averted, but Parvati insisted that Shani look at baby Ganesh to give a proper blessing. When Shani did look at Ganesh, the baby's head promptly fell off. In desperation, Ganesh's father, Shiva, replaced the baby's head with the nearest head he could obtain, which happened to be that of a ceremonial elephant.

Ganesh has the power to transcend the mind, which is why he is a symbol of spiritual wisdom beyond intellect. Although Shani can impose immense hardships, these challenges lead to powerful spiritual evolution for Saturn types. In the case of Ganesh, a horrible event precipitated a spiritual trans-formation that resulted in an archetype worshipped by billions of people over millennia. Saturn's lessons always serve to wake us up to our deeper spiritual nature, though the events are often horrible, such as disease, loss, pain, hardship, and turmoil.

As with Shani's character, Saturn types are hard workers with focus, determination, and the ability to persevere through hardship. They are will-ing to be patient and take the long road, recognizing the fleeting nature of instant gratification. Saturn types are happy to stay in the background and silently serve others without expectation of reward or recognition. They can handle immense responsibility and are usually the most mature in their age group. They are also not afraid of commitment and can commit to a person, project, or lifestyle for the long haul. This makes them highly disciplined, and they can be monklike in their spiritual practices.

Shani's brother is Lord Yama (also a child of Surya's shadow wife, Chaya), who is the god of death and dharma (cosmic law). Yama transports you to heaven's gate when your time is up. Shani is also the boss of Chitragupta, the celestial accountant who shows you your karmic balance sheet at the pearly gates. This makes Saturn an accountant of both time and karma, doling out what is due at the right time. (You can see why Saturn rules karma, dharma, death, and taxes.) Saturn is not mean by nature, but rather a partner through life, standing by your side, delivering various challenges in order to purify your karma, and improving your balance sheet in preparation for the moment you get to heaven. So although Saturn's lessons are tough, they serve to evolve your soul.

This mindset of paying back what is owed alludes to the karmic balancing algorithm constantly in the back of a Saturn type's mind, wanting to punish those who do wrong by cosmic law. They have a strong sense of justice, enforcing what is right and wrong in a sometimes cruel way, honoring principles over people. They prioritize rules over caring about the person involved. They are also very time conscious, and have little compassion for those who are even just a few minutes late to an appointment.

Saturn types are the ultimate organizers. They have strong attention to detail, they understand the interrelated nature of systems and people, and they are also good at deciding the rules and policies needed to ensure good, efficient functioning. They can be frustrated with inefficient processes and want to reorganize things. They are hard workers, even preferring the clothing of the working class: jeans, canvas, and rough cloth, and often worn and shabby. They may also value old things, such as used clothes and antiques—because Saturn is connected to old age and time—preferring to use something until it is worn out before discarding it. They loathe wasting anything. They are masters at extracting the most usefulness out of people and things and make great organizational managers. They excel at research and science and are willing to do all the hard work it takes to discover the truth. And they will stand by the truth, even if it hurts.

While a Venus type might rely on charm, Saturn types rely on deep technical knowledge and experience to navigate life. They are also willing to make the unpopular decision. In contrast to the Moon, who cares about feelings and what people think, Saturn cares more about doing the right thing, even if it is unpopular. A balanced Saturn type provides discipline, focus, and persistence, but an out-of-balance Saturn type can often feel left out or scorned by society, as Saturn himself experienced with his father. In their most powerful form, Saturn types are disciplined monks, silently finding the divine through quiet contemplation and meditation.

QUALITIES OF A STRONG SATURN TYPE

- Has a strong sense of right and wrong. Is willing to stand up for truth and justice.
- Is not concerned about popularity, but about getting the job done.
- Can be determined, focused, and persevering.
- Is well organized, with good attention to detail.
- Has discipline. Is time bound and honors commitments.
- Focuses on the problem, rather than the person behind the problem.
- Is a hard worker. Is serious and likes to work alone.
- Has high expectations of performance.
- Can be introverted and also insensitive to the needs of others.
- Often has gaunt, striking features.
- Relates to the working class over birth-right status.
- Likes the colors black or blue, and likes to wear clothes of the working people.
- Is a natural accountant. Has a strong sense of right and wrong. Is justice oriented, but in a cosmic way (conscious of dharma).

Rahu and Ketu (North and South Lunar Nodes)

Rahu and Ketu are the *chayagraha* (shadow planets), due to their mysterious nature. Though they have two distinct personalities, we must start by understanding how they are related to each other. They are the hardest planets (and people) to understand, reinforced by the fact that they are not even visible in the sky; they are points in space where lunar or solar eclipses take place.

Eclipses can occur either during a full Moon or new Moon, depending on the alignment of the Earth, Sun, and Moon. A lunar eclipse can happen during the night of a full Moon, when the Earth's shadow blocks the Moon's light from the Sun. A solar eclipse can happen during the day of a new Moon, when the Moon casts its shadow across the Sun, blocking its light from our Earth perspective. The alignment of Earth, Sun, and Moon during an eclipse happens at two specific, opposing points in space, known as the lunar nodes in Western astrology or the umbra in astronomy (the Latin word for *shadow*). In Vedic astrology, the north node is known as Rahu and the south node as Ketu. They don't really exist, physically speaking, which is why they're known as shadow planets. On a subtle level, they cast a shadow on our personality and in areas of life that they occupy in our birth chart.

The legend goes that there was a great war between the Devas and the Asuras. During this war, the Asuras were gaining the upper hand, and it was beginning to look hopeless for the Devas. In desperation, the Devas approached Supreme Lord Vishnu for help, claiming that the impending rule of the Asuras would completely unbalance the universe. Vishnu advised that the only solution would be for the Devas to obtain the nectar of immortality so that they could never be defeated. The challenge was that this nectar lay in a pot at the bottom of the vast, milky ocean (immortalized as the Milky Way galaxy). It would take enormous effort to churn this ocean and thicken it enough to raise the pot. The Devas were too weak to do such churning on their own, so they formed a diplomatic pact with the Asuras, promising a share of the nectar. This alliance got ahold of a tall mountain, plopped it in the middle of the milky ocean, and wrapped the massive Asura serpent Vasuki (often seen coiled around Shiva's neck) around the mountain. The Asuras took the head of Vasuki, and the Devas, the losing side, got the tail end of the deal. As the two forces alternately pulled in opposite directions, the coiled serpent rotated the mountain and churned the milky ocean, creating a buoyancy that at first raised the highly destructive Halahala poison that threatened to destroy all creation. Lord Shiva came to the rescue and contained it by swallowing and holding it in his throat, turning him blue. (Shiva is often worshipped as Neelkanth, the blue-throated one). Once the poison was dealt with, various gems and deities emerged, including Lakshmi, the goddess of prosperity, whom Vishnu invited to be his consort. Finally, after much struggle, Lord Dhanvantari, the god of medicine, appeared, holding in one hand the scrolls of the Ayurveda healing system and in the other the pot containing the nectar of immortality.

As the Devas and Asuras gathered around to drink the nectar, Vishnu disguised himself as the lovely maiden Mohini and tempted the lustful Asuras away. They were led to Varuni, the goddess of wine, who instead served them an intoxicant from a replica pot, leaving them drunk and oblivious to the deception. The Asura Vasuki, being a clever serpent, saw through this ruse, avoided temptation, and instead disguised himself as a Deva so that he could sit and enjoy the real nectar. (In some versions of this story, the Asura Svarbhanu is the one who sees through the ruse, and only after he is cut in two are his separated head and body merged with serpent parts. As with any Rahu/Ketu-related situation, there is always confusion and ambiguity.)

As the real pot was passed around, various Devas, including the planets and stars, drank of the nectar to become forever immortalized in the heavens. Vasuki, in his disguise, managed to partake of the nectar, but the moment a drop of it entered his throat, the Sun and Moon, with their combined light and intuition, exclaimed, "He is an imposter!" Hearing their cries, Vishnu reappeared, and using his powerful discus (fashioned from some of the radiance removed from the Sun), chopped off the head of Vasuki. That single drop of nectar, however, had made him immortal, but now as two disconnected parts: a serpent head called Rahu and a serpent tail called Ketu.

Because the Sun and Moon were the tattletales, Rahu and Ketu vowed to destroy them. But without a complete body, there can never be success. We see Rahu and Ketu attempt to swallow up the light again and again during eclipses. The severed parts strive for revenge, but they only succeed in creating a temporary shadowing of the light, as the Sun and Moon reappear from the disassociated parts.

This epic mythological story explains the shadowy, obsessive-but-intelligent nature of Rahu and Ketu. Wherever they are in a birth chart, they become powerful karmic forces that can really make you lose your head. This story also explains the temptations that can pull us toward lustful behavior and intoxicants, confusing us from the real nectar of salvation. Rahu and Ketu form an axis across a birth chart that represents areas of life in which you will face your own churning of the ocean and eclipsing of your light. This churning initially brings up destructive poisons that need divine support to heal, but eventually you will find health, prosperity, and the nectar of spiritual liberation. As they say, struggle breeds strength.

Rahu is connected to obsessions and addictions because it is a head with no body, and so whatever it consumes, it never feels satisfied. Rahu is connected to fame, ambition, social media, and other forces that can make us lose our heads. Ketu is the tail of the serpent, unattached to feelings. Ketu is connected to endings and abrupt changes in life. Being without a head, it has the possibility of transcending the ego and renouncing materialism to become a highly spiritual energy. We must realize that, just as happens with an eclipse, it is nothing more than our own shadow obscuring our own light, and that the light is always there to be found.

Rahu and Ketu are the outcastes of the court. They are the outlaws and the rebels and the disrupters, constantly trying to unseat the king and queen (Sun and Moon). They can also be dishonest, but not always for the wrong reason, as in the tale it was the Devas who were dishonest with the Asuras.

Rahu ☊

Rahu types think differently and uproot old conventions and limited ways of thinking, possessing an expanding energy that gets bigger and bigger until it blows up. They are the innovators who come up with revolutionary ideas that destroy the old ways. They are not easily put in boxes, and they often go against the grain of society. Rahu types can be larger-than-life figures, but they get caught up in chasing fame and recognition. They may have naturally addictive and obsessive personalities and give in to drugs or other escapist tendencies, where they end up confused about what is true. This can manifest more positively as becoming actors or social media influencers. Rahu types are constantly busy, with so much going on that they lose their heads. They have a strong sense of urgency and want to get everything done at once. They also want to experience every possible thing in life, but as the Rolling Stones would say, they "can't get no satisfaction." In Sanskrit, a *bhogi* (the opposite of a yogi) is someone who always indulges in pleasures and experiences rather than disciplining themselves. Therefore the materially oriented bhogi is often associated with Rahu imbalance. You might see Rahu types greedily acquiring more things, eating more food, consuming more intoxicants, and lusting after more people, in line with the tendencies of the Asura from which Rahu came.

They can, however, be powerful innovators and out-of-the-box thinkers, disrupting old technologies. Many entrepreneurs and inventors display Rahu tendencies to defy convention, though they typically get obsessed with their company or invention. It is said that there's a fine line between a genius and a mad person. Rahu types flirt with that line.

QUALITIES OF A STRONG RAHU TYPE

- Is constantly seeking change and stimulation.
- Can be compulsive, obsessive, and lustful.
- Finds life to be overly busy.

- Wants to experience as much as possible in the shortest amount of time.

- Has a restless nature.

- Easily falls into addictive patterns with work, people, or substances.

- Can be deceitful (remember how Vasuki tricked the gods).

- Can be confused about the right path in life.

- Can find it challenging to manage and control their lives.

- Is usually unorthodox, unconventional, eccentric, and innovative.

- Is an out-of-the-box thinker.

- Can be very ambitious, craving fame and fortune.

- Can be overly confident and full of themselves. (Rahu is all ego.)

Ketu ☋

Ketu types, as the flip side of Rahu, are people who are not obsessed and instead walk away from things they don't want to follow. They defy convention, work outside the rules, and innovate by tearing down what exists (rather than blowing it up, like Rahu types would). You could call them reductionists. They can also be very selfish and self-serving, not caring about others because there are no head and heart here. They are also powerful spiritual renunciates, leaving the world behind and preferring to meditate in silence and in solitude. Ketu types also tend to shun materialism and can live in a very austere and simple way. Many great saints are Ketu types, once they learn to connect their lower and higher natures.

QUALITIES OF A STRONG KETU TYPE

- Likes to go against the norms of society.

- Does not care for fame or fortune.

- Prefers to be silent, alone, and aloof. Can be antisocial.

- Keenly feels losses in life, such as jobs and relationships.

- Does not have strong self-confidence. (Ketu, with its head cut off, has no ego.)

- Lives an unconventional lifestyle. Does not care for a regular nine-to-five job.

- Is happy to lose it all and walk away from fame and fortune.

- Can have powerful spiritual abilities as well as psychic and clairvoyant abilities. Transcends the material world.

- Makes a good practitioner of the occult. Well suited to being a natural medicine healer, astrologer, energy worker, shaman, or yogi—in other words, people who transcend religion.

Rahu and Ketu are also associated with the Kundalini forces discussed in yogic texts. Kundalini energy is often described in yoga as a serpent energy residing at the base of the spine. When activated, this energy rises from the root chakra at the tailbone (Ketu the tail), up the chakra system to the crown chakra (Rahu the head), reuniting the Kundalini serpent and providing a flow of the nectar of immortality associated with liberation, or *moksha*. This creates the power to outsmart the gods, as Vasuki did. Though Vasuki is a demonic serpent, he is submissive to Shiva, wrapped harmlessly around his neck. Shiva was the original yogi, who taught a system of techniques that can bring Asura energies under control.

The negative manifestations of these energies can range from lust, greed, anger, pride, and jealousy to outright criminal behavior. When these energies are brought under control, however, this leads people to ultimate evolution, symbolized by the tamed Vasuki around Shiva's neck. If Rahu and Ketu are managed, the reconnecting of the head and tail is equated with the Devas and Asuras from the myth working together, showing how we must work with both our lower material and higher spiritual natures to find true happiness. Ketu types are naturally drawn to occult and nonconventional spiritual practices, whereas Rahu types only come to such practices after things in their life get chaotically out of control. Wherever there is chaos, there is an opportunity for spiritual advancement.

Leveraging the Vedic Planetary Archetypes in Life

We have covered the archetypical and energetic character of each of the nine planets used in Vedic astrology. We are all a combination of all these archetypes, because they were all present in the sky at the time of our birth. A trained astrologer can look at a birth chart and see if any of the planets are exerting an outsize influence on a person's personality. However, you don't need an astrologer to see the recognizable personality traits in yourself and those around you. Once you have a sense of the archetypes and stories described, you will naturally notice how they show up in people and in situations in your life. As you pay more attention, you may catch one or two traits related to a planetary archetype, and then see further traits of that archetype reveal themselves.

We all know people that strongly fit one of the archetypes, but typically we are predominately some combination of two or three of the archetypes. Events around you also clearly connect to these energy archetypes. Attending a powerful and inspiring leadership speech would be Sun energy, while seeing an accident or someone speeding by might be Mars making himself known. Someone caring for you could be the Moon, while love and romance or a show of wealth is Venus energy. If you get lost in social media, or all of a sudden find lots of creepy crawling insects in your home, or have issues with addictions or obsessions, there is Rahu. Loss, challenges, or obstacles are easily connected to Saturn. A Ketu type might show up as antisocial and unconventional, while someone showing up wearing a green shirt rattling off statistics and data is a clear manifestation of Mercury. A learned person with high degrees and perhaps a generous spirit is Jupiter showing up.

You can also notice a deficiency in the planet energies. A shy or low-self-esteem person might be lacking Sun energy, and a person without discipline or work ethic is lacking Saturn energy. Not being able to stand up and fight for one's beliefs shows a lack of Mars energy, while not being able to communicate clearly is a Mercury challenge. Not finding love in life is a lack of Venus energy, while not finding good teachers is a Jupiter challenge. As you observe the world around you, you can categorize personality traits and events as being strong or weak energetic manifestations of the planets. An astrologer analyzing a birth chart does just this, evaluating how each planet is showing up in someone's life, and advising them how to increase or decrease the energies as needed for better balance and harmony in life.

Now that we understand the personalities of the planets, we can begin to better understand the underlying energies of the zodiac signs because each zodiac sign has a specific planet that lords over it. So rather than sign-based astrology thinking, we are examining a more planet-based approach to understanding our lives.

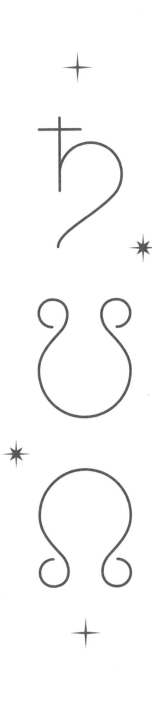

CHAPTER 7

The Vedic Sky:
Your Soul's Chart

Your rising sign, accurately calculated to a real position in space, is a major determinant of your personality at a deeper soul level of your being. However, rather than obsessing about the sign itself, in the Vedic system we see the signs as expressions of the planets. The Sanskrit word for *constellation* is *rashi*, which translates as *a collection of energies*. The word sign suggests it is symbolic, which is consistent with the symbolic calculation used in Western astrology. When we use a correct calculation, constellation is a better term and relates to the idea of a collection of energies. I will continue to use the word sign, however, for colloquial convenience.

Each rashi is said to have a planet that rules or lords over the sign, and the personality of that planet expresses itself through the energy field of the constellation (see Fig. 4). Therefore, understanding the planet ruling a sign becomes more important than the sign itself. Rather than identifying as a Virgo, a Vedic-oriented person would identify more with the personality of the lord of Virgo, who is Mercury, and then understand how Mercury gets modified through Virgo.

Each zodiac sign is associated with one of the five natural elements, considered in Vedic tradition to be the building blocks of nature—fire, earth, air, water, and space (space is where all the signs reside and is the only element not associated with specific signs). By combining the planet ruling a zodiac sign with its associated element of nature, we can better understand the energy of a given sign and how it influences a person. For instance, Mercury, the young intelligent prince, has two signs: Virgo and Gemini. Virgo, being an earth sign, brings out the more practical, earthy-oriented nature of that intellect, whereas Gemini, being an air sign, brings out a more airy, creative, but less practical nature of that intelligence.

The Vedic birth chart is essentially a diagram of the sky at the moment you were born, and is known as a *horoscope*, which comes from a combination of the Sanskrit word *hora*, meaning *time*, and the English *scope*, meaning *observation*. This snapshot of the heavens is attached to (remember the word *lagna*) and centered around a person's unique rising sign, so each rising sign produces a different birth chart (see Fig. 5).

Once the zodiac constellation on the eastern horizon is determined, it demarcates a section of sky that gets assigned as a First House, or starting point, of an individual's birth chart. The remaining zodiac constellations, going around the sky in a circular fashion, continue on from that First House. The sky gets divided up into a total of twelve sections, each ruled by a zodiac constellation (and planet), and each assigned a house number counting from the First House.

Each house has a zodiac sign influencing it, based on whatever that rising sign was. Each of the twelve houses is associated with a particular area of life, including personality, finances, love, children, and career, and each determines the energy present in a specific aspect of life. As described earlier, the section of sky east of the birth point influences personality. The house that's directly overhead from birth influences how we show up in the world, and is known as the House of Career, the Tenth House. As we count back from the eastern horizon to the Fourth House—the section of sky directly below the Earth, hidden from view—we come to the House of Mind, which determines our hidden psychology. Opposite the eastern rising House of Personality is the western setting House of Partnership, the Seventh House, which determines how we relate to other people. Each of the twelve houses corresponds to twelve key areas of life, as shown in the example of a North Indian–style horoscope in Fig. 6.

THE RASHIS

ZODIAC CONSTELLATION	RASHI	PLANETARY LORD	NATURE ELEMENT	KEYWORD	SYMBOL (FORMATION)
Aries	Mesha	Mars	Fire	Energetic	Ram
Taurus	Vrishabha	Venus	Earth	Stable	Bull
Gemini	Mithuna	Mercury	Air	Dual-Natured	Male-Female Couple
Cancer	Karkata	Moon	Water	Nurturing	Crab
Leo	Simha	Sun	Fire	Commanding	Lion
Virgo	Kanya	Mercury	Earth	Pure	Maiden
Libra	Tula	Venus	Air	Balanced	Weighing Scale
Scorpio	Vrishchika	Mars	Water	Intense	Scorpion
Sagittarius	Dhanus	Jupiter	Fire	Moral	Archer
Capricorn	Makara	Saturn	Earth	Practical	Crocodile
Aquarius	Kumbha	Saturn	Air	Unique	Water Pot
Pisces	Mina	Jupiter	Water	Adaptable	Twin Fish

Figure 4

BIRTH CHART ALIGNED TO THE SKY

EXAMPLE OF A GEMINI RISING

This constellation influences the Tenth House.

OVERHEAD

10TH HOUSE

PISCES

9TH HOUSE

11TH HOUSE

AQUARIUS

ARIES

Sun
Constellation /
Sun Sign

8TH HOUSE

12TH HOUSE

TAURUS

CAPRICORN

WESTERN HORIZON

7TH HOUSE

SAGITTARIUS

GEMINI

1ST HOUSE

EASTERN HORIZON

Rising
Constellation /
Rising Sign

6TH HOUSE

SCORPIO

CANCER

2ND HOUSE

Moon
Constellation /
Moon Sign

5TH HOUSE

LIBRA

LEO

3RD HOUSE

4TH HOUSE

VIRGO

UNDERGROUND

Figure 5

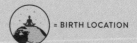

= BIRTH LOCATION

A Vedic astrologer assesses each of these houses and uses the sign ruling them, as well as any planets positioned in those locations, to understand the type of energy and personality that shows up in that specific area of life. We all have multiple personalities that emerge depending on the area of life in question. Perhaps we are bold and aggressive when it comes to our career, but emotional and nurturing when it comes to our relationships.

A Vedic birth chart shows where zodiac constellations were in the sky, based on the particular rising sign, and then assigns house numbers to the various zodiac signs. This helps us understand what type of energy is prevalent in different areas of life, based on that particular birth moment for that individual. Overlaid on this diagram are the locations of various planets in the sky, which the astrologer can then interpret to assess what energies of planets and signs are influencing different areas of life. By understanding the nature element of the sign in a particular house, we can also understand the type of energy involved. For instance, a fire-based sign signifies a fiery, aggressive energy, a water-based sign indicates more emotions, and an earth-based sign indicates groundedness. An air sign signifies an airy and intellectual quality.

We all have all signs in our birth charts or horoscopes. Every sign, whether you like it or not, shows up in one of the twelve houses of your birth chart, and so that personality shows up in that specific area of life. In a way, you have to root for *all* the signs, because each one shows up somewhere in your life. By being overly attached to one sign, you may be ignoring key energies in the other eleven areas of your life. The rising sign, or the First House, is known as the House of Personality, and so that single section of sky on the eastern horizon has the most influence on your overall personality. Using a Vedic chart calculator (which can be found at astrology-decoded.com) you can easily determine your rising sign.

That sign will have a certain elemental quality: fiery, watery, airy, or earthy. However, each sign in Vedic astrology is ruled by a specific planet, known as the lord of the sign. In the case of the lord of the rising sign (the First House), it becomes the planetary lord of the entire chart, and the most important planet for you to be aware of. Depending on where that specific planet is placed in your chart, it can determine the focus or theme of your life. For example, if the lord of your chart is in the Tenth House, the House of Career, you will be a career-oriented person; your personality may be defined by the work you do. If the lord of the chart is in the Fifth House, the House of Creativity, your creative output or your children may be more of a defining factor.

In Western astrology, we might use a zodiac sign to label a person's personality. However, through the Vedic system, because we understand this concept of a planetary lord, we need to take into account how strong that lord is before we can assess personality. We cannot narrowly focus on the rising sign, because the expression of that sign is attenuated by how strong the lord of that sign is. So if that lord of the chart is strong or weak, it will affect how similar or dissimilar you are to that specific sign. For instance, the sign of Leo is ruled by the Sun and is a fire sign, and as we learned about the Sun wanting to be the center of attention, a Leo-rising person would have a lot of that Sun energy and be quite strong-willed—provided they have a strong Sun in their chart. If they shy away from attention and are not strong-willed but are a Leo-rising sign, we would then know that they have a challenge with their Sun energy being weak. So if they are a Leo-rising sign, the Sun is the planetary lord, and based on knowing their observable personality, we can determine if that planetary lord is strong or weak.

As another example, someone whose rising sign is Cancer, which is a water element, would naturally be a nurturing and emotional person. Cancer is ruled by the Moon. If the Moon is strong in the chart, the person will be similar to the typical description of Cancer. However, if the Moon is weak (for instance, if it was waning and dark at the time of birth), or is in a difficult position in the chart, or even placed in a zodiac sign that the Moon is not happy in, then the person would have fewer Cancer-like traits, or perhaps unstable emotions.

Analyzing all this requires a competent astrologer with solid analytical skill and intuition. What we want to cultivate, however, is a self-awareness that does not rely on an astrologer's chart interpretation. As with all Vedic

NORTH INDIAN–STYLE BIRTH CHART

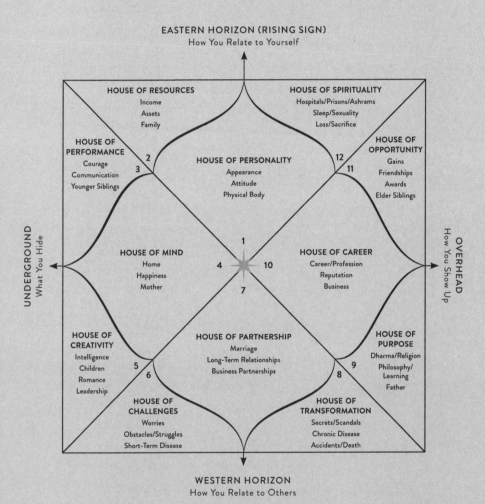

EASTERN HORIZON (RISING SIGN)
How You Relate to Yourself

UNDERGROUND
What You Hide

OVERHEAD
How You Show Up

HOUSE OF RESOURCES
Income
Assets
Family

HOUSE OF SPIRITUALITY
Hospitals/Prisons/Ashrams
Sleep/Sexuality
Loss/Sacrifice

HOUSE OF PERFORMANCE
Courage
Communication
Younger Siblings
2
3

HOUSE OF PERSONALITY
Appearance
Attitude
Physical Body

12
11
HOUSE OF OPPORTUNITY
Gains
Friendships
Awards
Elder Siblings

1

HOUSE OF MIND
Home
Happiness
Mother
4   10
7

HOUSE OF CAREER
Career/Profession
Reputation
Business

HOUSE OF CREATIVITY
Intelligence
Children
Romance
Leadership
5
6

HOUSE OF PARTNERSHIP
Marriage
Long-Term Relationships
Business Partnerships

9
8
HOUSE OF PURPOSE
Dharma/Religion
Philosophy/
Learning
Father

HOUSE OF CHALLENGES
Worries
Obstacles/Struggles
Short-Term Disease

HOUSE OF TRANSFORMATION
Secrets/Scandals
Chronic Disease
Accidents/Death

WESTERN HORIZON
How You Relate to Others

⁎ = BIRTH LOCATION

Figure 6

systems, we can improve our own self-awareness to better understand and improve ourselves, leveraging the archetypes presented in this book. By knowing our rising sign and understanding the traits of that sign, and then assessing how similar we are to that pattern of energy, we can know if we are a strong expression or weak expression of that sign's energy. Based on that strong or weak expression, we can then determine if we have a potentially weak planet ruling the rising sign of our birth chart.

Out of all the planets, the one that rules your chart is the most important. If the lord of the chart is weak, the whole chart gets affected, impacting all areas of life: health, wealth, relationships, career, and others. By focusing on understanding the lord of your chart and assessing how strongly or weakly it shows up, you can develop a very targeted and efficient approach to improve your whole life. Our goal here is to understand your rising sign, its planetary lord, and how aligned you are to that sign and planet, and then make lifestyle changes targeted at that planet to improve everything in your life.

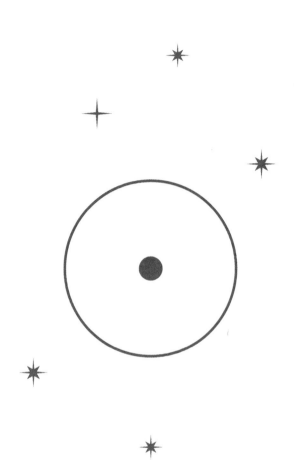

CHAPTER 8

The Vedic Zodiac: The Stars That Showered Your Arrival

Let us now examine each of these zodiac signs through the lens of the planetary lord. Once you find your sign and assess how you show up versus the prototypical sign, ask yourself: Are you showing up as a balanced version, or perhaps an exaggerated or a repressed version of that sign?

Leo (Simha) Rising Sign—Ruled by the Sun

Just like the planet that is bright, shining, and front and center, Leos (with a strong Sun ruling them) are bright, shining, and like to be the center of attention. Being a fire sign, that fire creates a strong-willed, natural leader with strong personality and character. Fire also correlates to the energetic nature of Leos, as well as the light they shine in social situations. They both are noticed by others and enjoy being noticed. As the lion symbol connected to Leo, they set high standards as king of the jungle and know well how to navigate hierarchies and aim for the top of the food chain, caring about recognition, prestige, and honor. They are naturally independent thinkers and inspiring people, generating their own light. They typically have bold ambitions and can have powerful vision into the future (in connection with how far the light of the Sun travels).

As the king of the court, they have a noble, regal presence and can become overly proud or arrogant (if the Sun is very strong in the chart). As with the story of the Sun, they may make difficult partners with their excessive light. They also set very high standards for themselves but get dejected like a lion with its tail between its legs when they fail. As the Sun makes its own light, Leos are supremely self-confident, but that fire can get out of hand (as the story of the Sun relates) and burn people. Leos can make powerful speeches and have a commanding voice and presence. A Leo-rising person who has weak Sun energy in their chart would struggle with these described traits and would have to try to increase the fire element in their lives.

> **Keywords:** Authority, recognition, pride, leadership, independence, vitality, and warmth.

> **Exaggerated Leo:** Too much ego, not considerate of others, self-centered, and vain. Continual need for more power and attention. Delusional visions of grandeur and constant need for recognition.

> **Balanced Leo:** Natural leader, loved by all, shines in social situations. Understands how to leverage structure of organizations and institutions. Visionary but practical.

> **Repressed Leo:** Weak willpower, shy, does not feel seen and recognized. Challenges with leading and with leadership figures. Not able to formulate long-term vision.

Cancer (Karkata) Rising Sign—Ruled by the Moon

The nurturing and loving nature of the Moon shows through Cancer, a water sign that is connected to maternal energy. The water element connects to tears, which makes Cancer types highly emotional. They have strong emotional intelligence, and prefer to connect with others on a heart level, exchanging feelings rather than dry ideas. Cancers like to take care of others and like to be taken care of; they are both nurturing and need nurturing.

They have a devoted nature and are usually friendly and naturally oriented to taking care of their family and even treating their friends like family. Cancers also love their home and love to host and entertain at home. Cooking is a natural expression of a Cancer person's love, as is finding comfort in food. They are also highly sensitive to the feelings of others, and as the Moon's light is a reflection of the Sun, their moods are easily influenced by those around them. They can acutely tune in to the moods of the masses, sensing what is going on in the zeitgeist.

Because the Moon waxes and wanes, Cancers can have their moods wax and wane as well. They are intuitive, sensitive, and, similar to their symbol, like to be around water. They can also exhibit a hard and tough exterior like the crab to protect their sensitive nature underneath. Cancers might lack self-confidence because they are so dependent on the light of others. They can be softer and more gentle in their speech, and know well how to tailor their delivery to their audience.

Keywords: Nurturing, sensitive, domestic, emotional, feeling, intuitive, and family.

Exaggerated Cancer: Overly emotional, mood swings, too sensitive, and overly influenced by the energy of others. Does not like to leave the home.

Balanced Cancer: Warm, nurturing, intuitive, and perceptive. Sensitive to the needs of others. High emotional intelligence.

Repressed Cancer: Not getting enough nurturing and not able to nurture others well. Overly defensive and protective and does not share their emotions. Poor intuition. Hard time letting go of troubling emotions. Insecure and defensive.

Aries (Mesha) and Scorpio (Vrishchika) Rising Signs— Ruled by Mars

Mars is the warrior planet, but when expressed through the two signs it rules, we can see how the sign's element shifts the expression of its personality. Aries is a fire sign, while Scorpio is a water sign.

ARIES (MESHA)

Aries are headstrong and stubborn, fighting to get their way. Indeed, the ram symbol illustrates the head-butting nature of an Aries. As a fire sign, they can be hotheaded, rash, and aggressive. In balance, Aries are action-oriented and courageous, as is the warrior Mars. They love adventure and new conquests and put a lot of energy into their pursuits. They are independent, self-oriented, and like to get things done. They take initiative and are good at starting new things. *Act first, think later* is their motto, and they can often be impulsive. They are usually very direct and precise in their speech. They are naturally competitive and push themselves and others to achieve results and goals. They also make great athletes and have well-developed muscles.

In their pursuit of goals, they can be insensitive to others, and with the fiery Mars energy, they can run hot and be hot-tempered. Their minds, however, are very sharp with piercing intellect and they are usually quick thinkers. They are also happy to enforce rules upon others, having the Mars militaristic trait of the commander in chief, and happy to debate and argue their strategic point of view. Out of balance, they can be ruthless, domineering, and hot-tempered, while a weak Mars exhibits an inability to set and accomplish goals or shows a lack of courage and willpower.

> **Keywords:** Strong, pushy, headstrong, action-oriented, initiating, courageous, quick, impulsive, and hot.

> **Exaggerated Aries:** Hot-tempered, angry, domineering, ruthless, and impulsive. Aggressive and competes with everyone.

Balanced Aries: Courageous, independent, action-oriented, and takes initiative. Accomplishes goals, clear and direct in speech. Adventurous and dynamic in nature.

Repressed Aries: Afraid to take action, fearful, does not stand up for beliefs. Unable to accomplish things. Unable to get to the point. Fearful, conservative, and shy.

SCORPIO (VRISHCHIKA)

Scorpios share many of the Mars attributes of Aries, but as a water sign, they are much more emotional. The scorpion symbol alludes to Scorpios wanting to stay hidden and in the background, while the water element shows the strong emotions lurking under the depths. If you push a Scorpio too hard and their emotions get triggered, they will sting, and that can be lethal.

Scorpio is the most intense, mysterious, and secretive sign, but Scorpios are brimming with deep intelligence. They are fascinated with what is hidden, so they are great at investigating and researching, and given their mysterious nature, they can be drawn to learning about occult and mysterious topics such as astrology and transformational psychology. They are also good at keeping secrets and thus make good spies and soldiers. Their Mars nature also leads them to happily use force when necessary to achieve their objectives; while you might see an Aries charging at you, Scorpio is more a master of the surprise attack. With strong watery emotions, Scorpios are very passionate and sensual and can also become very spiritually oriented, diving into the more esoteric and occult side of things. Their speech doesn't always express how they really feel, but with powerful emotions, they can really move people through their words.

Keywords: Hidden, secretive, mysterious, intense, seductive, and investigative.

Exaggerated Scorpio: Cunning, plotting, and overly intense. Uncontrolled emotions and rage. Does not reveal true self even to close friends. Psychologically complicated and insensitive to the needs of others.

Balanced Scorpio: Good researcher and investigator. Drawn to alternative healing systems. Passionate, sensual, and sensitive to psychology and emotions of themselves and others. Good balance of logic and emotions.

Repressed Scorpio: Insecure, paranoid, emotionally vulnerable. Poor logic that is overshadowed by emotions. Unable to get past setbacks. Obsessive and jealous of others.

Gemini (Mithuna) and Virgo (Kanya) Rising Signs— Ruled by Mercury

Mercury, the bright, intelligent young prince of the court, shifts depending on the airy influence of Gemini or the earthy influence of Virgo.

GEMINI (MITHUNA)

In Geminis, Mercury has a full expression of its intelligent nature, because the air element is connected to intelligence and thinking. They are naturally curious and like to explore, both in terms of information and knowledge. Geminis are full of energy, and are constantly moving like their lord, Mercury. They love change, activity, and dynamic work. They think very quickly and are great at absorbing information and spouting facts and trivia. They are great with communication and technology and love to post on social media. They have a natural love of learning and thinking through different ideas, though they can get overly lost in logic and thought, almost airy and lofty in their ideas.

The Vedic symbol for Gemini—a man and a woman together—shows how Geminis are flexible and open-minded in their thinking, allowing them to see two perspectives at the same time. However, this open-mindedness can also make then indecisive, paralyzed by their analytical skills and unable to tap into deeper intuition. Their flexibility shows up both physically and mentally. They can easily adapt as needed to different situations. They often possess an experimental and curious sexual nature. They also love to act, play, sing, and dance and enjoy keeping things light. They don't like to get too serious. They love to have an exchange of ideas and can be very charming and eloquent in their speech. Geminis easily make friends, and like the young prince Mercury, enjoy playing with those friends. However, with too many friends or too much stimulation, they can become neurotic or overstimulated, because they possess a very excitable nervous system that can easily go out of balance. Geminis need to retreat once in a while and take quiet rest to calm their nerves, but then they can get restless if their airy nature is too contained; lots of balancing is required for Geminis.

Keywords: Quick-thinking, intellectual, communicating, adaptable, and flexible.

Exaggerated Gemini: Neurotic, overly talkative, and easily overstimulated. Not well grounded. Overloaded with information and cannot make decisions. Highly changeable mind. Unable to sit still, racing thoughts.

Balanced Gemini: Likes to learn, good with facts and trivia, and strong rational thinking abilities. Open-minded, considers all the facts in decision-making, logical. Expresses themselves easily, both through writing and speaking.

Repressed Gemini: Not able to process information or handle too much information and ideas. Overly accommodating. Not able to think clearly or make logical and rational decisions. Lack of motivation and interest in learning or being social. Unable to express themselves.

VIRGO (KANYA)

Mercury expresses itself through earthy Virgos in a more practical way. Whereas Geminis have lofty ideas, Virgos are more practical and grounded. They also have strong intelligence and intellect and can absorb a lot of facts and information. Virgos are the most perfectionist of the signs. They care about order, details, and cleanliness. Any kind of profession that requires attention to detail or a steady hand, such as craftspeople and surgeons, fits Virgos well.

The maiden as its symbol connects to purity, protection, and service. Virgos can be very strict about their diet and keeping themselves and their environment clean. They can also set very high standards and be hard to please. Their strictness can be hard on others, and they constantly worry about things that are not in balance or in order in their own lives. They have a strong service mindset, wanting to help others. As with the young prince Mercury, they are quite physically oriented and enjoy physical activities, which combined with their strictness and attention to detail makes them very good athletes and yogis. Their speech is informative and precise, though they still possess the playful energy of Mercury.

> **Keywords:** Precision, detail, strictness, high standards, perfection, and analytical.

> **Exaggerated Virgo:** Overly critical, judgmental, and strict with others and themselves. Perfectionist with exceedingly high standards. Obsessive about order and detail. Constantly worried about things going wrong. Works too much.

> **Balanced Virgo:** Good attention to detail, orderly and organized, and balanced in thinking. Service-oriented mindset with strong intelligence and ability to organize facts and information in a practical way. Works hard and likes to be in service to others. Pure minded.

Repressed Virgo: Poor attention to detail, not able to make sense of information and facts, disorganized and impractical. Unable to express themselves clearly. Does not work hard. Messy and disorderly.

Sagittarius (Dhanus) and Pisces (Mina) Rising Signs— Ruled by Jupiter

Jupiter, the ultimate teacher, shows up differently through the fire sign Sagittarius, almost having a fiery, preachy, religious quality, versus watery Pisces, which has a more expansive, fluid, and spiritual nature.

SAGITTARIUS (DHANUS)

In Sagittarius, Jupiter's high ideals of morality, truth, and pursuit of knowledge are well expressed. Sagittariuses have good morals and a religious and philosophical bent of mind. They have a strong sense of principles and justice and can have strong opinions. Being the celestial priest, Jupiter likes ritual and tradition, which Sagittariuses can be very drawn to. They like to follow the strict protocols for ceremony and religion, and can be overly rule-based and conventional. They lean more toward religion than spirituality, wanting definition rather than exploration.

The fire element of this sign can make Sagittariuses hot-headed in their ideals, becoming self-righteous and sometimes forcing people to follow their dogma (remember Daksha Prajapati excluding his daughter and son-in-law). They can have an authoritative and persuasive voice to convince people of their ideas. They can also be so focused on the rules that they lose sight of practical matters (remember Brihaspati losing Tara by being too focused on his rituals). In balance, Sagittariuses like to have fun, have a generous spirit, and like to be with friends. As Jupiter is a heavy planet and expansive, Sagittariuses can get lost in overindulgence and fun. The symbol is an archer carrying a bow, signifying the strength and targeted conviction of Sagittarius. It also alludes to their athletic ability.

Keywords: Philosophical, idealistic, moralistic, fair, religious, conventional, and judgmental.

Exaggerated Sagittarius: Elitist, close-minded, not accepting of different belief systems, overindulgent, self-centered. Dogmatic and impractical. Fiery conviction that their way is the only way. Highly opinionated and self-righteous. Will pursue goals at the expense of others.

Balanced Sagittarius: Moral, fair, philosophical, and knowledgeable. Loves learning and is kind, generous, and religious. A natural teacher, valuing higher education. Has clear goals.

Repressed Sagittarius: Not interested in learning and knowledge. Not generous, warm, or giving. Selfish and introverted. Does not have any opinion and can lack a moral compass or be unclear on their values and goals.

PISCES (MINA)

With Pisces, we see the watery and emotional side of Jupiter. Pisces are sentimental and easily moved to tears and can have large and intense emotions (expansive Jupiter combining with watery emotions). With their watery nature, they can flow everywhere, often having trouble setting appropriate boundaries for their emotions, their speech, and the people in their lives. They can sometimes be unclear, using many words but not describing anything. They often lack practicality in their approach to life.

The spiritual nature of Jupiter, beyond dogma and religion, shows up in Pisces, who are expansive thinkers with a spiritual, contemplative, and philosophical disposition. They have powerful intuition and can easily find universal wisdom in all spiritual and religious paths. They can have big ideas and impossibly lofty ideals, wanting all of humanity to be uplifted. The boundary-setting challenge for Pisces also shows up in grandiose ideas and an expansive imagination, which can be impractical and unclearly defined. They are generous, friendly, kind, and giving, but can sometimes lack self-confidence. They can also be prone to overindulgence (both Jupiter signs have this tendency of expansiveness when it comes to food and fun). The symbol of two fish swimming in opposite directions shows that Pisces are dependent and influenced by their environment, but also may be indecisive.

> **Keywords:** Intuitive, spiritual, mystical, generous, kind, expansive, imaginative, emotional, boundaryless, and impractical.
>
> **Exaggerated Pisces:** Overly emotional, lacking boundaries, ungrounded, and impractical. Lost in ideas and unable to implement them. Doting over others. Overindulgent and prone to addictions. False sense of abundance. Can lack compassion for others.
>
> **Balanced Pisces:** Intuitive and spiritual in nature. Friendly, expansive, and generous. Compassionate nature makes people feel good around them. Powerful imagination and wisdom, good at teaching, and interested in acquiring knowledge. Good advisor, listener, and counselor. Sympathetic to others. Feels a sense of abundance and connection to the divine.
>
> **Repressed Pisces:** Unable to connect with others. Gives and receives poor advice. Feels a sense of scarcity. Poor imagination and not interested in learning new things. Does not like to indulge themselves or others and can devolve into self-pity. Not able to surrender to a higher power.

Taurus (Vrishabha) and Libra (Tula) Rising Signs—Ruled by Venus

Venus, the planet connected to love, sensuality, harmony, and beauty, shows up in a more worldly form in the earth sign of Taurus, while it's more idealistic and intellectual in the air sign of Libra.

TAURUS (VRISHABHA)

In Taurus, the Venus energy shows up as an appreciation for beauty, art, and music, though combined with the earth element, it takes on a practical and often materialistic nature. Venus being connected to wealth and money makes Tauruses good earners. They easily start accumulating things to reward themselves for that hard work. Given that they are drawn to the finer things in life, this may show up as collecting art and luxury goods and a strong attachment to status symbols of wealth. Their Venus nature also makes them very sensual and romantic. The bull symbol, connected to plowing the earth, sowing seeds, and harvesting the fruits of that work, makes Tauruses good at earning, investing, and building wealth (the bull symbol is a sign of success in the stock market).

The bull and Earth are also connected to stability, and Tauruses are stable, steady, and resolute, though this can be to the point of stubbornness, because a bull can be hard to get moving. But once the bull gets going, that perseverance shows, like in the hard work it takes to plough earth. Tauruses are hard workers who also enjoy working with their hands and connecting with the Earth through nature. That earthy nature also makes them want material security on the Earth plane. They are drawn to knowledge (remember, Venus was also a teacher), music, and dance, and are typically good teachers and communicators, as well as good advice givers on practical matters and finances (remember that Venus is the advisor and treasurer of the court).

Keywords: Stable, steadfast, strong, cautious, luxury-seeking, productive, and resolute (bull-headed).

Exaggerated Taurus: Stubborn, fixated on materialism, addicted to luxury. Lost in sensuality and overly pleasure-seeking. Uses intelligence only for material pursuits, greed, and gain. Jealousy and dissatisfaction with their material wealth. Can't let go of possessions and emotions.

Balanced Taurus: Good advisor on practical matters. Hard worker. Appreciative of art and music. Firm and balanced approach to materialism and personal growth. Good love and romance in life, and harmonious relationships. Overall happiness and contentment.

Repressed Taurus: Poor financial state, poor relationships. Lacking in both love and abundance. Disharmony, discontent, and unhappiness. Lacking in sensuality and appreciation of the arts and music.

LIBRA (TULA)

In Libra, the air element adds an intellectual energy to Venus, making for a person drawn to high ideals around justice, fairness, and universal harmony. The symbol of the weighing scales (similar to the scales of justice) shows the harmony- and balance-seeking nature of Libras. This ability, along with good advising skills (remember that Venus was the court advisor), make Libras natural leaders who can ensure the balance of different ideas from different people. This also makes them good at commerce, business, and handling money in general, in line with the weighing scales, a symbol of trading and business in ancient times. They are drawn to defend a higher truth and higher ideas, but in their own striving for balance, they are conflicted between the material world desires of Venus and the higher ideals from their airy nature. They can be very inspiring, charming, and charismatic, and have a natural power to influence others toward a higher cause.

Their Venus nature makes them love beauty, art, drama, and music, and Libras like to be in beautiful surroundings, surrounded by beautiful things and people. They can also be good at art and music. They are also social, enjoying parties and gatherings, especially if they are more refined and luxurious events. Their social nature, combined with their skill at forming partnerships, makes them naturally good at business, networking, and generating wealth. This partnership-forming skill also makes them very diplomatic, like Venus's role in the celestial court as the advisor and diplomat.

> **Keywords:** Balance, harmony, mediator, peace, beauty, weighing both sides, partnership, business, and luxury.

> **Exaggerated Libra:** Uses charm to take advantage of others. Overly materialistic. Lofty ideals that are not connected to reality. Falls in with the wrong crowd. Gets lost in hedonism and social indulgence.

> **Balanced Libra:** Good at keeping the peace. Socially oriented. Forms good relationships. Appreciative of the arts and music. Able to create harmony in teams and groups. Strong ideals.

> **Repressed Libra:** Lack of beauty and abundance in life. Lack of balance and harmony in work and relationships. Not able to appreciate music and arts. Unhappy and isolated.

Capricorn (Makara) and Aquarius (Kumbha)—Ruled by Saturn

Saturn, the planet of discipline, hard work, and the working people, expresses itself through a more practical way in the earth sign of Capricorn, and in a more intellectual way through the airy sign of Aquarius.

CAPRICORN (MAKARA)

Capricorns are the practical, hard-working, organized, and disciplined people that persevere through any type of challenge. Being an earth sign, they are highly practical and methodical and like systems that are organized and efficient. They can be highly focused, as is Saturn's nature, but with that can come a coldness and distant mechanical efficiency. They like schedules and clear plans, but can be more focused on the numbers and the goal than the feelings and the people. They make good organizational leaders in industries where systems and processes matter.

Because Saturn is also quite lonely and distant, Capricorns prefer solitude and enjoy working alone, unencumbered with having to deal with what they would consider the inefficient emotions of others. Their practical intelligence outweighs their emotional intelligence. Because Saturn is connected to old age, Capricorns are drawn to old things and old places, such as antiques and historical sites. The crocodile—the symbol for Capricorn in Vedic astrology—represents patience. Capricorns can move in a very measured way toward their long-term goal. They are also good at hiding their true feelings and ambitions, just like a crocodile hides underwater. Their earthy nature, however, makes them quite stubborn and hard to convince to change direction. Their speech is usually clear and practical, and can be dry and to the point rather than flowery and emotional.

Keywords: Stability, security, caution, practicality, worker, and focus.

Exaggerated Capricorn: Cold and calculating. Overly conservative and cautious in decision-making. Focused on accomplishments and material success. Workaholic that prioritizes work over fun. Cruel logic. Cares more about results and the work than about the people. Cold, distant, and stubborn.

Balanced Capricorn: Practical, organized, and diligent. Has good focus and is conscious of time. Dependable, reliable, and disciplined. Works efficiently and is a hard worker. Good manager of people and processes. Has patience to achieve long-term goals.

Repressed Capricorn: Poor time management, lack of discipline, and impractical. Not organized or efficient. Scattered thinking and unable to focus. Lack of determination and persistence.

AQUARIUS (KUMBHA)

For Aquarius, an air sign, the intellectual nature of Saturn comes through as a champion of the working people (remember, Saturn is the servant of the court). Aquariuses are humanitarian in nature, always trying to lift up the downtrodden. They tend to put others above themselves and can sometimes become quite self-deprecating, believing in others more than they believe in themselves. With the Saturn energy they can be quite negative, but when channeled the right way, they can easily surrender to higher causes and a higher divinity. They have tremendous patience and can even mimic Saturn in their slow movements.

Saturn is also connected with going against the grain, and Aquariuses can be eccentric and follow different societal norms. In fact, they can be very innovative in coming up with new ways of thinking. Their patience also lends itself well to fields such as research and investigation, where a long-term focus is required. The airy nature of the sign, combined with the nature of Saturn, gives Aquariuses the ability to take an abstract concept and organize it in a practical and useful way. They're often good at applied science, technology, and innovation. The symbol of the water pot suggests that they also enjoy water, and can hold many secrets in their mind, keeping certain things hidden. They also have the tendency to keep their true feelings and emotions hidden. Their speech can also be slow and measured, taking a while to get to the point. They typically struggle with charisma and charm. They also rebel against hierarchy and the elite, wanting everyone to have a fair shot.

Keywords: Humanitarian, unconventional, eccentric, servant-like, and secretive.

Exaggerated Aquarius: Eccentric and does not relate to others. Rebels against the mainstream. Secretive and stuck in a fixed mindset. Hidden feelings and slow to take action. Lacking in charm.

Balanced Aquarius: Humanitarian and cares for the downtrodden. Innovative and creative. Willing to go against the grain. Patient and can take a long view to success.

Repressed Aquarius: Lost in impractical ideals. Not a hard worker. Lacking in patience. Too much of a follower. Does not respect hierarchy or organizations. Lacking in organizational ability.

Rahu and Ketu

Rahu and Ketu, the two shadow planets, do not have true ownership of any of the zodiac signs, fitting with their outcaste status. However, they play powerful and important roles in a birth chart. As shadowy and eclipsing forces, they create turmoil wherever they are in the chart. Being a head and a tail, they are always opposite from each other, and they form an axis of imbalance where work is needed. For example, it might be the axis of work-life balance or the axis of honoring yourself versus your relationships. This analysis is complex and confusing (due to the confusing nature of these planets), however, you can often easily identify which two areas of life you are working to find balance in based on your lived experience. Wherever the head is, you might find an excess of intensity that you need to learn to manage, and wherever the tail is, you might need to learn to let go of attachment.

If either Rahu or Ketu are in your rising sign (which means the other node would be in your House of Partnership), that would cause those energies to show up in a big way in your personality and relationships.

Based on opposing houses in a Vedic birth chart (see Fig. 6), there are six areas of life that could have Rahu-Ketu challenges. These are the typical karmic areas of imbalance as examined in Vedic astrology:

- Sense of self versus relationships with others: First House—Seventh House axis.

- Self-reliance versus dependence on others (for example, family): Second House—Eighth House axis.

- Practical work versus deeper purpose and meaning: Third House—Ninth House axis.

- Personal life and peace of mind versus career and work: Fourth House—Tenth House axis.

- Children and creativity versus accomplishments and recognition: Fifth House—Eleventh House axis.

- Obstacles and health challenges versus spirituality and liberation: Sixth House—Twelfth House axis.

A full analysis of these opposing karmic themes would necessitate deep analysis, but you may recognize the natural struggles we all have with them. Should Rahu and Ketu heavily affect any of these axes, it can cause lifelong challenges (churning) that require a deep spiritual approach to overcome.

Influences on the Rising Sign

If you have identified your rising sign, that information—combined with an understanding of that sign's planetary ruler—helps you partially understand your true personality at a soul level, underneath all the conditioned layers of your upbringing and society (and perhaps pop-culture astrology). Depending on the strength of the ruling planet in your chart, you may see an overly exaggerated manifestation of the sign's attributes, a healthy correlation, or those attributes struggling to manifest. By knowing your Vedic sign, however, you have a compass to help guide you toward your innate, balanced personality. By leaning into your true nature, you strengthen the lord of your rising sign, which, being the lord of the whole chart, strengthens all areas of your life. Honoring your innate personality helps improve your whole life.

A further influence of energies comes from any planets that are in that rising sign at the time of your birth (any planets showering your birth from the eastern horizon), because the energy of those planets will have an outsize effect on your personality from that location. So though you may be a Cancer rising who is emotional and nurturing, if aggressive Mars is positioned in that house, it will color everything red. That aggressive and hot energy will now influence the Cancer personality—meaning the nurturing, mothering nature is there, but possibly tinged with rage if it isn't reciprocated. If Rahu or Ketu are sitting in that rising sign, then those unconventional characteristics will show up, with Rahu adding an obsessive and outsize quality to the sign's personality, and Ketu adding a sense of aloofness and self-negation, or a spiritual dimension, to the sign's personality.

Some planets in a chart also influence other houses through a concept known as *drishti*. As many yogis practice when doing a balancing pose, this refers to an intense gaze at a specific point. So an Aries rising who is aggressive and intense can be tempered in that aggression with the drishti, or gaze, of comforting Venus onto that First House. There can also be a planet somewhere else in the chart (not in the rising sign) that due to its strength and intensity can imbalance the whole chart with its influence. Analyzing drishti and its effects on various aspects of a chart takes years of experience to understand. However, through your personal experience of yourself and others, you will sense any planets with outsize influence on a person's personality. An obsessive person likely has some strong Rahu influence, whereas a ruddy-faced, temper-prone person probably has Mars influencing their personality. Someone who is ultra-organized and time-bound likely has Saturn influencing their First House.

Therefore, rather than focusing on only your rising sign and its planetary lord, it is important to use your powers of self-observation to understand what planets are most predominant in your natural experience of life. Noticing aggressive tendencies (Mars), discipline (Saturn), harmony (Venus), over-thinking (Mercury), issues with authorities (Sun), challenges with nurturing (Moon), or over-indulgence (Jupiter), you can assess how strongly and how balanced various planets are showing up in your life. With this observational approach, blended with an energetic understanding of your rising sign and various planets, you can begin to have more awareness and take targeted steps to balance and harmonize those energies. This can give you more alignment and ease through life, without requiring a professional astrological analysis.

CHAPTER 9

Finding Karmic Balance through Remedies and Rituals

A fundamental differentiator of Jyotish is the vast system of karmic remedies for challenges and imbalances in life. While your Western sign might be
an interesting talking point, without the backdrop of a karmic understanding, it's nothing more than a casual self-assessment. With your Vedic sign,
you have not only a tool for deeper self-awareness but also a compass with
which to make and navigate powerful shifts in your life.

The Vedic system, as a whole, is the ultimate tool for human development and spiritual evolution. The Vedic birth chart gives you a map of the
territory of your life, showing you strengths, weaknesses, challenges, and
opportunities. The ancillary Vedic systems surrounding Jyotish provide
a rich and varied set of remedial approaches to tackle any challenges or
weaknesses seen in a chart. The sister sciences of yoga and Ayurveda
contain some of the most powerful remedies to improve life and, when
employed with the targeted understanding derived from an accurate birth
chart, can enable miraculous results.

A Vedic astrologer can, for instance, diagnose the root cause of a mysterious disease and then suggest a range of approaches from the physical
(such as visiting a doctor, running some blood work, or performing physical exercise) to the emotional (such as working with a psychologist or

therapist, or journaling) to the karmic (such as using yogic techniques to settle mental disturbances) to even the magical (such as balancing planetary energies through specific rituals and mantra practices). It all depends on the level of consciousness of the client and their willingness to put in effort for healing. A jyotishi can employ tools from yoga, Ayurveda, or the Vedic system of mantras (specific sound vibrations and chants), pujas (fire-based rituals and worship), yantras (spiritual geometric patterns), archetype and deity worship, and gemstone and color remedies.

A jyotishi examines a person's birth chart, assessing various planetary strengths and weaknesses and, in consultation with the client, learns about various challenges. The jyotishi then tries to determine the root karmic and planetary cause of that challenge, and then, leveraging their intuition, creativity, and personal practices, devises remedies to balance out the karmic issues. Karma is like a debit or credit account. Every action you have ever taken, good or bad, over multiple lifetimes has a consequence and must be paid back. It's like the saying, "What goes around comes around."

Recall our restaurant analogy from chapter 2: The chefs, servers, suppliers, landlord, bus staff, and host all collaborated to enable your pleasant experience, but now you owe all those people. If you walk out of the restaurant without paying, that karmic debt will likely catch up with you. Perhaps you'll receive a knock on your door from the police and be subjected to a court case or fine. To avoid that challenging payback, you have some options: You can use cash to pay for the meal, write a check, swipe a credit card, or if you have no means to pay you may have to wash dishes to cover the debt. In life, however, the debt that is due from a past life experience and the various payment methods are not as clear. What debt did you incur in a past life? Did you pay it back previously? Is something still owed? And what methods can you use to pay it back now?

The Vedic astrologer is able to analyze this karmic debt and figure out more pleasant ways to pay it back. For example, somebody may have some karma in their chart to go through a loss of income (perhaps they caused income loss for somebody in the past). One remedy might be to proactively change jobs (because leaving the first job would be a temporary loss of income, taking care of that debt), and another might be to mentor younger folks in their career, helping them improve their income, thereby balancing out the income-loss karma.

It is up to the creativity of the astrologer and contextual understanding of the life of the client to determine appropriate and approachable remedies. Sadly, some modern astrologers have resorted to only giving remedies that make them more money (creating their own bad karma). For instance, an astrologer might identify a challenge in the chart and then conveniently offer to sell a gemstone or suggest a ritual that they will perform for you for an exorbitant fee.

The best remedies, however, involve the effort and work of the clients themselves. Rather than just passively wearing a gemstone or having someone else perform some ritual, by making conscientious efforts in your life, you can have far more effective results. Without getting lost in the complex analysis of myriad planets, signs, planetary strengths, and areas of life, we will focus on the key planet in your life—the planet that rules your chart (the lord of your rising zodiac sign). That one planet lords over the whole chart, and because of that, it affects all areas of your life. By understanding the template of the typical expression of your rising sign and its planetary lord, you can easily intuit how strong or weak that planet is showing up in your life. If you strengthen that chart lord, it raises the strength of your entire chart and therefore your entire life. As they say, "A rising tide lifts all boats."

A planet is not by nature trying to cause you harm; it is merely an agent of karma delivering what your soul needs in order to evolve in this lifetime and pay back karmic debts. It's just doing its job! Therefore, rather than being fearful of any planet, we must understand that it is serving our soul. By propitiating or harmonizing its energy, we can pay back karma we owe in a more pleasant way. Though a planet may feel like an abstract concept, it is the rich mythology of Jyotish that helps us personify that planet and thus channel our human intelligence to harmonize and balance that planet's energy.

For minor imbalances or challenges in life, a remedy focused on the planet that rules your chart can shift things easily into balance. For more serious challenges, a deeper analysis into your chart by a competent, sincere, and insightful astrologer is needed to find the root cause of the challenge and collaboratively develop an effective remedy. However, with your basic understanding of planetary personalities, you can try a few remedies and look for signs (synchronicities and coincidences) to confirm that you are on the right track. We are essentially trying to satisfy the karmic debt collectors (the planets), and when they are happy with our approach, they usually let us know. Once you start a remedy, typically within days you will get some sign that encourages or discourages you to continue. It can be a serendipitous encounter with a person that signifies that planet's energy, an email with a related subject matter, a news story or social media post that pops up on your feed, or even a symbol, dream, or image that appears in your life. Of course, the more observant and mindful you are, the more you will notice these guideposts.

As you read through the remedies organized by planet, try to assess how that planet is showing up for you, and whether its energy needs increasing or decreasing. Try to incorporate the remedy, practice, or lifestyle change for at least forty days (provided you get early signs that you are on the right track), and then assess if things have shifted. Your goal is to live a life where you are conscious of these nine energy archetypes and actively manage them by appropriately increasing or decreasing their energy to enable a life of flow, balance, and soul satisfaction.

For any of the planets, one of the simplest remedies you can do is chant the mantra of that ruling planet 108 times at sunrise on the day of the week that is ruled by that planet: the Moon mantra on Mondays, the Mars mantra on Tuesdays, and so on. (Why 108 times? Twelve signs multiplied by nine planets gives us the highly auspicious Vedic number of 108.) As mentioned in chapter 3, the planets are known as grahas that grasp you at the causal level and affect your life. However, when you chant mantras, it is like you've covered yourself in slippery ghee, and so they have a harder time grasping you. You can also experiment with wearing the color of clothing for that planet on its specific day to help channel and harmonize its energy.

Sun (Surya)

Mantra: Om Suryaye namaha (*om sur-ya-yay nama-ha*)
Day of the Week: Sunday
Colors: Copper, red, orange, gold

The Sun is the powerhouse of our solar system, energizing our earth and lighting up all planets, so a weak Sun shows up as a lack of vitality and energy or poor overall health. If you are a Leo rising—with the Sun ruling your chart—and you are having self-confidence, self-esteem, or leadership challenges or problems with authority figures, your Sun energy needs strengthening. A simple way to do this is to spend more time in the Sun. Going out for a morning walk just after sunrise is an excellent Sun remedy that balances both a weak or strong (overly confident) Sun.

Anything connected to fire is also good to harmonize Sun energy. Lighting candles or oil lamps at sunrise or sunset, or sitting around a fire and looking into it are connections to Sun energy—after all, the Sun is essentially a ball of fire. Because the Sun is connected to willpower and leadership, making efforts to step up into leadership opportunities or exerting your will more often can help. Given that the Sun is the king—which in today's age are governments, corporations, and leaders—taking care of any outstanding issues with the government or solving any challenges with authority figures helps Sun energy.

The Sun is the father, so it can also be harmonized by taking care of your father, spending time with him, repairing your relationship with him, or even honoring your own fatherly responsibilities. If your father has passed, making charitable donations to organizations that are connected to governmental initiatives or elderly men can be good as well.

The gemstones for the Sun are garnet and ruby, and the colors are bright red, deep orange, and golden and copper yellow. Wearing these can also balance some of the Sun energy. If you find you are constantly the center of attention, then perhaps the Sun is too strong, so try to find more supportive roles and get out of your comfort zone. Conversely if you are avoiding the center of attention, try to exert yourself more and show up.

For yoga practitioners, a daily Surya Namaskar (Sun salutation), along with the twelve corresponding mantras, can be a powerful Sun harmonizing remedy that improves leadership, self-confidence, and digestive power. Following circadian rhythms by waking up around sunrise and winding down around sunset—and getting a good amount of sunlight into your home or office during the day—can also improve overall health. Even eating your veggies, as they are direct products of Sun energy, can help.

Copper is the metal connected to the Sun, so wearing copper, or letting water soak overnight in a copper cup and drinking it at sunrise, can harmonize and balance Sun energy. In India, this is known to boost the immune system. Gold is also a metal connected to the Sun and is worn by many cultures as a sign of overall prosperity, health, and well-being. Any of the main deities in India, such as Shiva or Vishnu, are connected to the Sun, because everything revolves around them. For other religions, the central figure, such as Buddha, Christ, or Allah, is connected to the Sun, so religious prayer or worship helps Sun energy. For advanced yogis, the daily recitation of the Gayatri Mantra (which should only be recited after instruction from a qualified teacher) is a powerful form of Sun worship, since Gayatri is the divine female form of the Sun.

Moon (Chandra)

Mantra: Om Chandraye namaha (*om chan-dra-yay nama-ha*)
Day of the Week: Monday
Colors: White, silver

In our solar day and age, when our workday, seasons, and calendar are oriented around the Sun, we have forgotten the power of the Moon and rarely pay attention to it. As an embodiment of the divine feminine, the Moon helps counter the masculine-dominated energy of the modern world.

Especially for a Cancer rising sign, it is important to pay attention to the Moon. Imbalanced Moon energy shows up as emotional challenges, poor intuition, difficulties in relating to or interacting with women, and a feeling of not being cared for. Take note of the full Moon nights, and stargaze on the new Moon nights. When the Moon is in the sky, meditate on it with an intense gaze and feel her healing rays. Then close your eyes and imagine that Moon in your mind's eye. For students of yoga, you can imagine the rays entering your Ajna chakra (third eye), activating your intuitive abilities and powers of perception.

Just as you know the month, date, and day, become aware of the Moon phase day, tracking its movement daily from new Moon to full Moon and back across its waning cycle. Attend full Moon rituals and gatherings, and start paying attention to the regular movement of the Moon across zodiac signs (using accurate Vedic positions). Because the Moon is connected to tides and water, swimming in lakes and oceans or just taking regular baths is good for harmonizing Moon energy.

Cancer is also connected to the home, so cooking at home, hosting at home, and entertaining others in your home is another excellent remedy. The Moon is also connected to politics, so joining a political cause or running for political office strengthens Moon energy. With the connection to the feminine energy, taking care of your mother—or women in general—or donating to women's charities, such as one focused on single mothers, can help, as can joining a women's circle (if you are a woman).

The gemstone for the Moon is the pearl (which you often see women politicians wear), and the color is white (the color that politicians in India wear). The metal for the Moon is silver, so wearing silver jewelry or drinking water out of a silver cup (especially if left overnight in the moonlight), can enhance your Moon energy. In India, feminine or motherly deities, such as Lakshmi (the wife of Vishnu) and Parvati (the wife of Shiva), are worshiped to honor the Moon. In the Catholic tradition, Mother Mary is connected to Moon energy, so I have often given Hail Mary recitations as a remedy for a weak Moon. Indeed, any kind of motherly nurturing—either being nurtured or nurturing others, honoring your motherly duties, spending time with your mother, or repairing your relationship with her—is a good remedy. Even recognizing the concept of the Divine Mother or honoring Mother Earth can enhance Moon energy. Sometimes, regularly receiving an oil massage is all it takes to fulfill that nurturing deficiency in life. Shiva is also connected to the Moon and Mondays, because he carries the Moon on his forehead, and so reciting mantras or chants to Shiva on Monday can be effective.

Mars (Mangala)

Mantra: Om Mangalaye namaha (*om mang-ga-la-yay nama-ha*)
Day of the Week: Tuesday
Colors: Red, maroon

Excess Mars energy usually shows up as anger, frustration, overconfidence, or judgment. It can also show up as blood issues, excessive accidents, or conflict. Scorpio and Aries rising will typically be strong at expressing their will and may be prone to anger, though Scorpio more slowly and hidden than headstrong Aries. To release some of that steam, Mars types will do well to exercise and get a sweat on, though competitive sports may aggravate Mars types' natural tendency to want to compete and destroy.

A weak Mars person—someone who is timid and fearful—should lean into being bolder and more courageous in their actions. They should also work on moving faster, because Mars likes to move fast (while overly strong Mars types need to slow down). Mars is a planet of getting things done, so executing tasks and projects honors Mars energy well. To strengthen Mars, it is better to take some decisive action rather than wallowing in indecision, which is against Mars's core philosophy of action. Mars is also connected to logic, engineers, and machines, and so any kind of fixing or repairing of physical objects, or any kind of problem-solving activity or strategic thinking, is harmonizing and soothing for Mars types.

Mars was nurtured in the womb of the Earth, so activities where you are connected to the Earth, such as barefoot walking and gardening, can calm down an overactive Mars person. Water and snow sports are also good options, as they evoke the cooling waters of Mother Earth that birthed Mars. Mars is also a warrior planet, so volunteering to help veterans or donating to veterans' causes can help you achieve balance. Mars is connected to the color red, but Mars types may become more hot-tempered when they wear red. A strong red should be used to strengthen a weak Mars type—for instance, if you have self-confidence challenges or lack courage. Lighter reds can calm an overly strong Mars.

The stone for Mars is red coral, especially the lighter, more pinkish variety, which comes from the cooling waters of the ocean. In India, fierce deities, such as Kartikeya and Durga, and warriors like Hanuman are worshipped to appease a difficult Mars. In yoga, the classic warrior pose is an excellent pose for calming Mars energy.

Mercury (Budha)

Mantra: Om Budhaye namaha (*om bood-ha-yay nama-ha*)
Day of the Week: Wednesday
Colors: Green

Mercury's signs, Gemini and Virgo, are connected to communication, so any kind of communication is helpful for Mercury, including therapy, talking with friends, writing, and journaling. Mercury out of balance shows up as poor communication skills, poor logical thinking, a lack of friendships, and a sensitive nervous system. Any kind of reading, writing, or communicating, as well as being playful or working with children or youth, is connected to improving Mercury. It is important to speak one's voice and express ideas in the physical plane, through the voice or written word, to keep Mercury happy and healthy. The teenage prince loathes not having his ideas heard.

Learning new things, figuring out new technologies, taking skill-building courses, and building practical skills all help Mercury, given that the prince is in his education years. It is important that Mercury types do not get too serious. So keeping things light, having fun, acting in a play, and reading for pleasure all settle and harmonize Mercury energy.

Too much Mercury energy leads to an erratic and neurotic disposition, so by sitting still and journaling or reading Mercury types can settle that energy—though too much screen time really affects the young Mercury. Mercury also likes to travel; taking trips, even short ones, are harmonizing for Mercury. Lightening up in life and not taking everything so seriously can also help. Playing games or participating in trivia nights is a natural Mercury activity. The prince is also quite athletic, so sports, athletics, and yoga are all good remedies. Yoga is especially powerful as a physical activity that calms the mind, combining two major attributes of Mercury the prince.

Because speaking is primarily connected to Mercury, mantra approaches work especially well. The power of sound is soothing for sound-sensitive Mercury. Mercury is connected to children, so donating to children's charities, reading to children, or donating books to schools and children's libraries is good for Mercury. Mercury's color is green, so using that color in clothing, wall colors, or decorations helps with intelligence and rational thinking. Mercury's stones are emerald, jade, and turquoise.

In India, the goddess of learning and education is Saraswati, and she is connected to Mercury. Vishnu is as well, because Mercury is full of charm, wit, and intelligence, as seen in Krishna, one of the key incarnations of Vishnu. Chanting either of their mantras is especially powerful for Mercury challenges. Vishnu has one thousand different names, so listening to each of them or saying them out loud is said to be one of the most powerful remedies in Vedic astrology. Vishnu is also said to have been the creator of Jyotish, and the overlord of all the planets and stars, therefore his worship is especially powerful in embodying Jyotish.

The name Budha is connected to Lord Buddha, the founder of Buddhism (who was also a young prince, prior to enlightenment). In the Vedic tradition, Buddha is seen as an incarnation of Vishnu, so any study of Buddhist philosophy, mindfulness practices, or chanting connects to Mercury. You can also see this connection in the jade bangles that many Buddhists wear.

Jupiter (Guru or Brihaspati)

Mantra: Om Gurave namaha (*om gura-vay nama-ha*)
Day of the Week: Thursday
Colors: Orange, yellow

Jupiter as a planet of wisdom and teaching is honored through any kind of higher learning or teaching. As its Sanskrit name Guru implies, it rules counselors, advisors, priests, and teachers, so interacting with any of these types of people, or engaging in those activities yourself, strengthens Jupiter, improving your own wisdom. As a coach and astrologer, I am blessed to be a source of Jupiter energy to many of my clients and students. Jupiter is the planet that provides knowledge, prosperity, and happiness, so it is an important planet for all people to nurture, and typically Jupiter-related professions help people with these themes. Conversely, a weak Jupiter shows up as a pessimistic outlook, bad luck, inability to create wealth, and overall misfortune, which causes people to seek out the above counsel.

Through the signs of Sagittarius and Pisces, Jupiter is connected to religion and spirituality. Exploring these things, visiting temples, churches, and spiritual places, as well as doing religious practices, all harmonize Jupiter energy. Because Jupiter loves rituals and worship, the ideal remedies for Jupiter types involve some kind of prayer, worship, or ritual. Simply honoring a daily ritual helps Jupiter energy.

Jupiter is the most beneficent planet of them all, so Jupiter remedies tend to improve overall happiness, health, and success in life. Jupiter is also very generous and kind, so displaying this behavior pays back dividends; Jupiter rewards generous people with many blessings.

Reading sacred texts, or any kind of philosophy, is good for Jupiter types, as is going to school to acquire more advanced knowledge, particularly degree programs. We all know the value of education in long-term wealth creation, which correlates with Jupiter's energy pattern.

The colors for Jupiter are orange and yellow, colors often worn by spiritual people in India and by priests. In Western culture, yellow is often seen as the color of happiness. The importance of turmeric and ghee in Indian culture, for both cooking and religious purposes, is another connection to the orange and yellow colors of Jupiter, which help overcome obstacles. Using turmeric and ghee in your food is a simple remedy for an imbalanced Jupiter. In India, we often put a spot of turmeric on our forehead and light ghee lamps at our altar to ask for Jupiter's blessings of happiness and health.

The stones associated with Jupiter are yellow sapphire, yellow topaz, and citrine. Making donations to institutions of higher education, or to temples, churches, synagogues, mosques, or other religious institutions, helps balance Jupiter energy, as does honoring priests of any tradition. Even a simple gift to a teacher strengthens Jupiter, as evidenced in the Western tradition of bringing an apple to your teacher (apples are connected to Venus, the other teacher).

Someone who has too much Jupiter energy may be too conventional or stuck in their thinking (remember Jupiter's dogmatic rituals), and so in this case, the person should explore being more open-minded, learning about different philosophies, and addressing practical challenges in life head-on. Jupiter can also be overly indulgent, so learning to have the right balance of discipline versus enjoyment when it comes to food is important. Jupiter, being the heavy one, is connected to the popular Indian deity Ganesh, who removes obstacles and has a big belly full of knowledge and big ears to listen and counsel well—all traits connected to Jupiter.

Venus (Shukra)

Mantra: Om Shukraye namaha (*om shook-ra-yay nama-ha*)
Day of the Week: Friday
Colors: Pink

Venus is a planet of beauty, luxury, and the finer things in life. Venus rules Taurus and Libra, so these signs should naturally enjoy those things, unless Venus is weak. Challenges with finances, relationships, your love life, and comfort in general point to Venus challenges. In that case, indulging in a few luxury purchases can be good to improve Venus energy. Visiting art galleries and attending fairs can also be good.

Venus is also connected to music and dance, so playing, listening to, and dancing to music are very good for Venus energy, as is indulging in your artistic hobbies. This can often lead to a state of transcendence as you sway in time to the music or lose yourself in your artwork. Venus is also connected to fun and enjoyment, so indulging in such things in a healthy way is good for Venus energy. Because Venus is also connected to money, having more fun improves that energy, too.

Too much Venus energy, however, results in too much hedonism and indulgence, which can then lead to imbalances with Venus, which ultimately cause unhappiness, loss of wealth, and challenges in relationships. This can also happen with overindulgence in luxuries and overspending. Being extravagant and wasteful can create negative Venus karma, eventually leading to financial hardship.

Venus rules romance, so ensuring that there is romance in your life, by dating or setting up romantic evenings with your partner, is an excellent practice to keep Venus in good balance. The stone for Venus is the diamond, which is connected to the Western idea of this stone signifying a commitment of love. Quartz is a substitute stone for Venus, and rose quartz can help with Venus energies like love and happiness. The color pink is associated with Venus, as are pastel colors. Dressing in your finest clothes honors Venus, and as the saying "dress for success" suggests, a nice wardrobe honors Venus and delivers success. The goddess Lakshmi in Hindu culture is connected to Venus, and is aptly known as the deity of wealth and happiness. Also, Saraswati, as the goddess of music and learning, is connected to Venus. Any feminine deity is connected to Venus energy, particularly deities associated with beauty, grace, charm, and happiness.

Saturn (Shani)

Mantra: Om Shanaischaraya namaha (*om shan-ace-cha-rye-ya nama-ha*)
Day of the Week: Saturday
Colors: Black, dark blue

As the planet of challenges, Saturn naturally has the most challenging mantra, but for Saturn, discipline and perfect practice is well rewarded. Saturn creates obstacles, restrictions, and karmic lessons in life. It can be the cause of gloom, depression, melancholy attitudes, and a life of constant hard work without recognition. On the flip side, it is the planet of discipline, focus, determination, practicality, and persistence. If you are Aquarius or Capricorn, you naturally have these traits with a strong Saturn, though that strength can make you melancholy. Weak Saturn energy shows up as a lack of focus, a lack of discipline, and being late to everything.

To harmonize the energy for Saturn, one must honor Saturn's character. Being on time for appointments and meetings, being disciplined in your lifestyle and diet, and practicing austerities such as fasting are all good to keep Saturn in check. Saturn is all about simplicity, so removing clutter and discarding useless items helps with Saturn energy. Saturn loves organization, and disorganization leads to Saturn being tempted to restrict and challenge you in life. Simply organizing everything, from closets to personal affairs, is a good Saturn remedy. Saturn is also connected to death and taxes (being Lord Yama's brother and Chitragupta's boss), so paying your taxes and getting your estate in order are smart ways to appease this energy.

Saturn is slow-moving, so taking your time to do things and cultivating patience helps avoid the injuries and carelessness that can result from Saturn being pushed past its speed limit. Walking at a slow pace is the ultimate Saturn remedy—especially barefoot on the earth—given that Saturn is connected to feet, legs, and slow modes of transport. Saturn is also connected to old things, so visiting ancient pilgrimage sites is a powerful Saturn remedy, further enhanced when you take the slowest mode of transport there (for example, a walking pilgrimage). Shoes and the dirt on them are connected to Saturn, which is why many cultures remove their shoes at home. Beyond hygiene, this is to avoid bringing Saturn's painful and restrictive energy into the temple that is your home.

The deity often connected to Saturn is Lord Shiva, because he is the epitome of discipline. He is often depicted in meditation; therefore, a disciplined, daily, quiet meditation practice is an excellent Saturn remedy. Practicing the eight limbs (branches) of yoga (as described in *The Business Casual Yogi* and other yogic texts), honors Saturn perfectly, because the limbs include discipline, restraints in behavior, meditation, and purification techniques. As mentioned earlier, Shiva is considered the original yogi.

Hanuman can also be worshipped to deal with difficult Saturn forces, as during the epic legend of the *Ramayana*, Saturn was rescued by Hanuman. The evil king Ravana captured the nine planets and carefully imprisoned them at specific locations within his house to create the ideal horoscope for himself. When Hanuman appeared, he rescued Saturn from his chains, who in return granted a boon that whoever worships Hanuman will be free of Saturn's bondage. Therefore, the many Western yogis who sing the *Hanuman Chalisa*, a song of praise of Hanuman's exploits, unknowingly receive Saturn's grace.

The stone for Saturn is blue sapphire, though wearing it typically isn't recommended, because it can bring a lot of hardship, particularly if one isn't living the life of an ascetic (Saturn is the lonely one). This was exemplified in Princess Diana, who selected a blue sapphire for her wedding ring, bringing much challenge and loneliness into her life (although you could also say that she accelerated her karmic advancement). So unless you are ready to take on a lot of challenges through accelerated karmic payback, it is best to avoid Saturn stones. Lapis lazuli is less powerful, and a lighter color could alleviate Saturn.

Blue clothes—especially rough, torn, or used clothing—is connected to Saturn. For instance, blue jeans are a typical Saturn person's piece of clothing. Simply pair your jeans with hard physical work on a regular basis, because Saturn is the ruler of manual labor. Without the hard work, such clothing only brings the restrictions and lost opportunities of Saturn into your life.

Saturn rules the working class, so supporting worker initiatives and taking care of the downtrodden helps with Saturn energy. Any kind of service to others, like volunteering your time or doing hard physical labor, is good for Saturn energy. Because Saturn rules old age and disability, helping an elderly person, or donating your time or money to elder-care homes or organizations that help disabled people, pacifies Saturn.

Saturn is also connected to science and research, so engaging in scientific-oriented tasks and research is helpful, as is any slow, thoughtful, data-based decision-making.

Rahu

Mantra: Om Rahave namaha (*om ra-ha-vay nama-ha*)
Day of the Week: Saturday
Colors: Brown, black, dark gray, purple, multicolored (variegated) patterns

Ketu

Mantra: Om Ketave namaha (*om kay-ta-vay nama-ha*)
Day of the Week: Tuesday
Colors: Beige, light gray (ash white)

The nodal planets do not directly rule any of the signs. However, if you have either Rahu or Ketu in your ascending sign, or if you experience increasing Rahu- or Ketu-like karma in your life, then it is important to calm those energies, because they typically create chaotic situations.

Rahu is connected to illusions, so being clear about your life's path and being realistic with your aspirations balances Rahu energy. Being overly ambitious, having delusions of grandeur, or letting popularity and fame get to your head are all signs of Rahu going out of balance. Rahu also rules addictions and obsessions, so managing those carefully before they get out of hand is important. Rahu tends to blow things up and create chaos. For instance, a clear sign of Rahu's influence is when someone gets extraordinarily famous but is not grounded, and therefore loses their head by falling into drug or alcohol addiction. Social media is another Rahu-exaggerating activity. Too much social media can create a lack of clarity and faith in yourself, because that imagery is illusory (remember, Rahu is a shadow planet). This can create an eclipsing Rahu force in your life.

Healthy Rahu activities include more balanced illusory activities, such as photography or using social media to further knowledge or support a good cause. Rahu is also connected to all intoxicants, so reducing drug use, alcohol, and other mind-altering substances is good for a Rahu type. As many addicts can attest, without a body, Rahu just keeps on consuming without ever feeling satisfied. That "can't get no satisfaction" phenomenon of Rahu can also result in workaholic tendencies or a constant state of busyness. Calming Rahu requires a clear-headed approach to work and proper prioritization of nonwork activities. With any kind of addiction or obsession, you can be sure Rahu is at play.

On the flip side, Ketu energy takes things away from you. Just as Rahu raises you up, Ketu takes you down. Ketu is connected to loss, unexpected change, and disillusionment. When you feel there is no point to your work or your life, then you know Ketu is acting up. Ketu is also connected to feeling lonely and disconnected. Ketu is, however, a very spiritual planet, connected to the mystical and yoga traditions. Ketu is balanced through spending time in silence, spending time away from people (for example, at retreats), and visiting spiritual sites.

Rahu and Ketu can be intense karmic forces. However, remember that Vasuki was very intelligent. He was the only Asura who saw through the ploy of the gods and even managed to trick the gods to gain access to the nectar of immortality. Therefore, Rahu and Ketu, when harnessed properly, give deep knowledge, wisdom, and perception, beyond even that of the gods. Rahu and Ketu exist outside of any religion or god, so any occult or nonmainstream (but healthy) practice helps Rahu and Ketu.

Yoga also improves Rahu and Ketu challenges, because it reconnects the severed head and tail via Kundalini energy along the spine. When the energies connect along the chakra system of the subtle body, the practitioner gains powerful yogic powers and enlightenment. Yoga and meditation are the ultimate remedies for Rahu and Ketu types, however poor guidance in yoga can lead to problems. As my yoga teacher describes, it can make people *lulu lemon* (lulu is Hindi slang for *crazy*, and paired with lemon, it sounds like a brand of yoga pants that people are crazy about). "Don't become lulu lemon with wrong yoga practice," he often says. The right practice of yoga brings out the powerful insight and otherworldly intelligence that Rahu and Ketu, reconnected as Vasuki, provide. As many a yogi will tell you, though, when they begin a serious yoga discipline, the first thing that comes up in their life is a churning of the Rahu and Ketu chaotic forces—almost as if to test their resolve—and a reliving of the milky ocean mythology. After this churning settles, a state of peace and enlightenment comes, much like the tamed snake around Shiva's neck. Rahu and Ketu are also the planets connected with psychic abilities, so people with such skills must be careful to not let those energies disturb them. Too much use of those abilities without proper grounding and guidance can lead to the Asura energies bringing chaos to the practitioner.

There are specific rituals and worship practices to manage difficult Rahu and Ketu situations, but they require trained practitioners to avoid getting on the bad side of Rahu and Ketu. A simple remedy, however, is burning a coconut oil lamp, because a coconut resembles Rahu—both as a head, and also since it's found at the top of the slender palm tree trunk, analogous to the crown chakra at the top of the spine. In India, coconuts are offered to temples as a peace offering to calm Rahu and Ketu. My Jyotish teacher—who is from South India, where coconuts grow in abundance—sees the coconut as representing our ego; it's a tough nut to crack. This is why offering a coconut in worship is symbolic of surrendering the ego. Lord Ganesh, because his head was also cut off, is associated with Ketu, while the fierce deities such as Durga and Kali are often connected to Rahu, the head itself. Durga and Kali are often cutting off the heads of Asuras in their mythology (which symbolizes the cutting away of the ego and its material desires in order to transcend into higher consciousness). Worship of these deities often alleviates chaotic Rahu and Ketu energies in life. Rahu and Ketu, being strange energies, require worshiping strange deities with strange rituals.

Because Rahu and Ketu together form a serpent, donating to snake habitats or visiting the snake enclosure at the zoo can work to balance this energy. Nag champa (meaning *flower of the snake*) incense used by many spiritual practitioners calms this energy as well. Incense typically starts out as brown and burns into white ash, symbolizing the brown color of Rahu turning into the white ash of Ketu.

Rahu and Ketu are also connected to our ancestors and those in our lives that have passed away. If you are obsessing over someone no longer with you, long after a healthy mourning period, this may be Rahu energy at play. You may face challenges in life due to decisions made and karma created by your ancestors, which points to Rahu and Ketu issues. By honoring your ancestors, learning about them, adopting forgotten family traditions, and performing rituals to propitiate those ancestors, you can not only move through grief but also pacify Rahu and Ketu energy, turning that energy into the blessings of your ancestors.

Stones and colors for Rahu and Ketu are not usually recommended, because they are unpredictable energies. They are best pacified through spiritual practices, mantras, and rituals. During those practices, hessonite garnet for Rahu or cat's-eye for Ketu can be involved. Once, when I did a ritual for Rahu and Ketu, the priest asked me to bring multicolored cloth for Rahu. Typically, the colors brown and purple are associated with Rahu (brown, the color of wood, is connected to the earthly and materialistic nature of the Asuras, and violet is the color of the crown chakra in yoga), while Ketu colors are light gray and ash white (which correlate with burning things to the ground for renewal). Folks with Rahu or Ketu challenges should use the above colors and stones with caution, being mindful of the energies they might be activating.

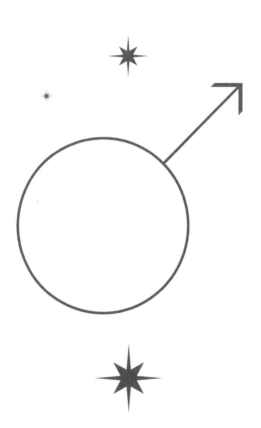

Conclusion

Through this simultaneous journey into the heavens and into the personality of your soul, you have been introduced to the ancient Indian system of Vedic astrology. As a primer, this book is but a dipping of your toes into the vast ocean that is Jyotish. You now have a basic framework to understand both yourself and others better, and you have hopefully developed a consciousness to tune in to and align with the cosmic rhythms. Start to observe your day-to-day existence and interactions and appreciate how the planetary energies pervade everything you experience. Start to relate various life events to the planets, noticing their workings through your karma. Look for energetic imbalances in your life and experiment with how to balance that energy through the framework of the planets, finding ways to manage that energy through the tools that you have learned.

If you decide to explore this subject further, it can become a lifetime (or several!) of discovery into the deeper concepts of Jyotish, getting into interpretations of the various houses of a chart, assessing the strengths of planets based on their location, and exploring the various representations and influences of planets in different areas of life. Beyond the basic planets and signs, the birth chart has a tremendous amount of deeper information. There are myriad subcharts or divisional charts, called *vargas*, which are mathematical derivatives of the birth chart to zoom into very specific areas of life, such as career, relationships, or children. There are also various planetary periods called *dashas* that show which planet is most active in your life at any given time. The vargas and dashas are powerful tools in Jyotish that have no parallel in Western astrology. When combined with *gocharas* (transits that overlay the current positions of planets in the sky onto your original birth chart), these tools give astonishingly insightful predictions of life experiences that can then be managed with highly targeted remedies.

Jyotish further divides the sky into twenty-seven sectors called *nakshatras*, which are star clusters related to Moon positions. Nakshatras give subtler and deeper insight into the influences on your life and connect to an even richer tapestry of mythology and remedies. There is also a massive branch of Jyotish known as *nimita*, the study of omens to interpret planetary energies from everyday occurrences, which helps to guide chart and life analysis. There's also the field of synastry, which matches the charts of two people to assess marriage or business compatibility and understand targeted areas to work on to ensure healthy relationships between those people. As you can appreciate, the possibilities and applications of Jyotish are endless and intriguing. For complex life challenges, a competent astrologer can help navigate an effective pathway toward healing and balance.

Through the various sciences of the Vedic knowledge system, you can learn to live in harmony with the cosmic law of the universe and to "live beautifully," as the jyotishi K. N. Rao described. Vedic astrology is a powerful system that helps you tune in to who you truly are. Through its power, you can avoid unnecessary detours in fulfilling your soul's purpose. You can gain powerful insight into why you are the way you are, why others in your life are the way they are, and why they show up in your life the way they do. Jyotish can also support your decision-making in all areas of life and help explain the root of challenges you are facing. It enables you to overcome obstacles more easily and live with more light, flow, and ease. I hope you continue your journey into the study of the light of consciousness that is Jyotish.

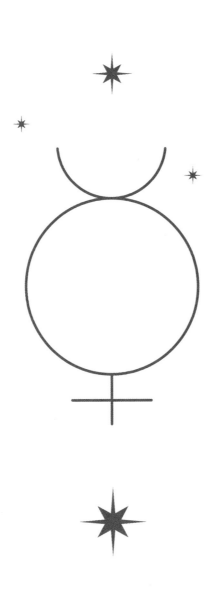

Afterword

Now that you understand the basics, you may want to approach a jyotishi for a formal reading to better understand your birth chart and manage challenges from a karmic angle. A jyotishi will analyze your chart to determine the very nature of your consciousness and various energies at play to give you pertinent advice to manage your life and karma better. Even if you do not know your birth time, a jyotishi can take the dates of various life events and triangulate all of that back to a fitting birth time, in a process known as birth time rectification. This itself is a testament to the power of the system.

Vedic astrologers are the ultimate karmic counselors; however, they too have their own karma (and their own charts), and it's important that you find the right astrologer for you, because you are opening your Pandora's box of karma to them. Some astrologers are highly computational, calculating all sorts of data and giving you an overload of information that may not be relevant. Other astrologers might have better bedside manners and really try to understand your human experience before relating that to what they see in the chart. Some astrologers may be focused on impressing you with their predictive ability, while others might focus on developing your personal self-awareness. They may also have a more spiritual view versus a more material, mundane worldview. It depends on the consciousness and spiritual outlook of the astrologer and the efficacy of their own spiritual practices.

With any astrologer, it's important that you assess whether they are sincerely in service to help and support you, out to make quick money, or just casual entertainment at a party or event. Do they have any other skills or training to add context to their astrological outlook? Their own personal experience might bias their interpretation of your chart. For instance, an astrologer who has never married or had children might have quite a different perspective on relationships and family than one who has. You will find that some astrologers specialize in family issues, health issues, leadership challenges, finances, or relationships, and have professional backgrounds ranging from medicine to psychology to business to investing. Cultural context can also be very important. A brilliant astrologer in India might not fully grasp the Western living experience. Conversely, a Western-born astrologer might not be as intimate with the ritual, mantra, mythology, and deity systems of Jyotish.

It is also important to note your chemistry with the astrologer. Do their affect and mannerisms resonate with you intuitively, or is there some karmic challenge between you and that astrologer that should be avoided? Their personality can be reflected through the planets. Do you want a more forceful, insistent Mars type, a diplomatic Venus type, or perhaps a more nurturing Moon type? You might also find strong-willed Sun types, heady Mercury types, doom-and-gloom Saturn types, advisory Jupiter types, confusing Rahu types, and renunciate, reclusive Ketu types. If you decide to work with an astrologer, really tune in to your intuition and assess whether that person would be a healthy fit for you. Even during a reading, gravitate toward interpretations that make intuitive sense to you, and learn to let go of advice that just does not feel right.

If you want to experiment with deeper remedies through the grace of the divine, you can approach the deities themselves for help and healing. In the ten-thousand-year-old Vedic system, a pantheon of deities provides easy ways to personify planetary energies. Each deity is connected to a planet, and by doing rituals and offering worship to that deity, you can channel your own energies in such a way that the planet behind the deity is propitiated. Though the ancient Vedic deities are mostly lost to antiquity, many of them have evolved and show up in the more recent four-thousand-year-old Hindu tradition. Some Hindu priests are highly attuned to the connection of planets and deities as energetic fields and can perform rituals directly to planets or the deities connected to them, occasionally with miraculous results. Most Hindu temples are also strongly aligned with Jyotish principles, sometimes having altars with statues depicting the nine planets themselves.

Through the maintenance of ancient rituals, temples are often energetic vortex points from which to powerfully shift karma, though the average modern Hindu often has no idea of this linkage, blindly following rituals without a clue as to the planets and karma behind them all. I have come across many a Christian, Muslim, Buddhist, or Jewish person who has visited a Hindu temple for an astrological remedy. The Hindu priests are only too happy to help (for their own karma's sake), and have no inclination to proselytize or ask for unreasonable fees (as that has a negative karmic consequence). The moment you talk about planets at a temple, you already have a more advanced perspective than the average Hindu visitor. The priest will likely be happy to oblige, and postritual you can observe any shifts in your life and decide if it was helpful. The priests will, however, ask you to take your shoes off to avoid bringing challenging Saturn energy into a place dedicated to easing karma.

Through the knowledge you have gained in this book, you can become a lot more aware of your life, your emotions, and your environment, and you can take a more active role in shaping them. You are the best observer and interpreter of your own life, and you are best equipped to tune in to your deeper nature, beneath all the layers of outside conditioning. By tuning in to this rich system of planetary energies, you will start to develop a relationship with the planets and automatically orient your life in accordance with your deeper soul rhythm. This alignment alone will help you gravitate to the right counselors, advisors, teachers, priests, and astrologers in your life to help you find even deeper meaning and flow.

Wishing you all the light, blessings, and grace of the navagraha. Hari om.

Acknowledgments

Thank you to my father for inspiring me with tales of our Vedic heritage, my mother for instilling in me a devotion to the Divine Mother, my wife, Kari, for activating my soul purpose as a teacher, and my children, Chetan, Jaya, and Dharma, for their love and light.

Gratitude to all the rishis, gurus, teachers, and students who have inspired my love of learning and teaching: Yogrishi Vishvketu, for illuminating my yoga path; Dr. Deepak Chopra, for my Vedic and Ayurvedic path; Dr. Suhas Kshirsagar, who opened the doorway to Jyotish and Vedic counseling; and Dr. Santhip Kanholy, who took me deeper into this study of consciousness and graciously reviewed this manuscript.

Thank you to the team at Mandala Publishing for their belief in my idea, especially to Phillip Jones, who from a chai chat around a planetary archetypes for leaders workshop suggested writing this book. Thank you to Katie Killebrew for believing in this project, and to Peter Behravesh and the editorial and artistic teams for shaping and crafting this into such a beautiful work.

Deep gratitude to the navagraha for their divine karmic guidance: the Sun for energy; the Moon for intuition; Mars for conviction; Mercury for writing; Jupiter for knowledge; Venus for financial means; Saturn for discipline; and Rahu and Ketu for access to the consciousness of Jyotish.

Quick Reference Guide

Planetary Personalities

SUN (SURYA)
Has a bright, shining personality with good energy, health, and vitality. Likes to be in charge, enjoys being the center of attention, and often has an orbit of people around them.

MOON (CHANDRA)
Has an emotional personality, strong intuition, and a caring, nurturing nature. Likes to connect at the level of heart, meaning, and feelings.

MARS (MANGALA)
Has a strong personality that can be forceful and aggressive. Likes to command and control to accomplish things. Bold, ambitious, and arrogant, and happy to debate, argue, or fight when needed.

MERCURY (BUDHA)
Is full of ideas, intelligence, and logic. Is usually very talkative, youthful, and playful. Enjoys using technology and communicating their ideas. Enjoys practical learning.

JUPITER (GURU OR BRIHASPATI)

Is wise and generous. Enjoys intellectual learning and is inclined to advising, teaching, and counseling others. Cares for tradition, ritual, and ceremony.

VENUS (SHUKRA)

Is charming, elegant, and graceful, and has an eye for art and design. Drawn to music, luxuries, trends, and appearances. Values material success and likes to visibly demonstrate it.

SATURN (SHANI)

Is disciplined, organized, and practical. Cares about principles over people and is very conscious of time and of doing the right thing. Values hard work and perseverance and doesn't care to flaunt material success.

RAHU

Has a compulsive and obsessive personality and often does not know when to stop. Is constantly hungry for more. Is an out-of-the-box thinker ready to blow things up for change. Has a large ego.

KETU

Is unconventional and likes to do things outside of the norm. Prefers to work alone and be away from others. Easily drawn to spiritual and occult practices. Can have too little ego, losing confidence in themselves.

Signs

ARIES (MESHA)—RULED BY MARS

Headstrong, aggressive, pushy, and domineering. Has strong drive and competitive spirit. Likes adventure and exploring new things. Can be impulsive and hot tempered.

TAURUS (VRISHABHA)—RULED BY VENUS

Strong, stable, and determined. Is steadfast, but can also be stubborn. Drawn to financial stability and security.

GEMINI (MITHUNA)—RULED BY MERCURY

Quick-minded, intelligent, and practical. Likes to communicate, is good with technology, and is open-minded and flexible.

CANCER (KARKATA)—RULED BY THE MOON

Emotional, intuitive and likes to connect from the heart. Sensitive, nurturing, and caring. Enjoys family and community.

LEO (SIMHA)—RULED BY THE SUN

Authoritative, proud, independent, energetic, and a natural leader. Likes recognition and likes to be noticed. Has high standards, but can also have a big ego.

VIRGO (KANYA)—RULED BY MERCURY

Has strong attention to detail and perfectionist tendencies. Prefers clean, organized, and pure things and has a mindset toward service. Analytical and drawn to precision and high standards.

LIBRA (TULA)—RULED BY VENUS

Likes to keep harmony and balance in relationships. Cares about justice and peace, and tries to weigh both sides of any decision. Is a natural mediator and peacekeeper. Enjoys luxury, beauty, and art.

SCORPIO (VRISHCHIKA)—RULED BY MARS

Has a secretive, hidden, and mysterious personality. Isn't easy to figure out. Can be intense and emotional, but also passionate. Drawn to researching and investigating things that are not commonly known.

SAGITTARIUS (DHANUS)—RULED BY JUPITER

Possesses a strong sense of morals and ethics. Drawn to religion and philosophy. Likes to honor convention and tradition. Can be idealistic but also overly judgmental to different ways of thinking.

CAPRICORN (MAKARA)—RULED BY SATURN

Is practical, hardworking, and determined. Has good self-discipline. Is practical and well organized. Is cautious in their approach to life, valuing stability and predictability.

AQUARIUS (KUMBHA)—RULED BY SATURN

Is a natural humanitarian, drawn to uplift the downtrodden. Intellectual in nature. Likes to come up with innovative, creative solutions to improve things. Out-of-the-box thinker.

PISCES (MINA)—RULED BY JUPITER

Is intuitive, spiritual, and mystical. Has an expansive, kind, and generous personality. Likes to learn and teach. Feels connected to the divine spirit. Can lack boundaries and be impractical.

Remedies & Rituals

SUN (SURYA)

Mantra: Om Suryaye namaha (*om sur-ya-yay nama-ha*)
Day of the Week: Sunday
Colors: Copper, red, orange, gold
Vedic Deities: Surya, Gayatri, Vishnu
Ritual Items: Fire, candles, oil lamps
Gems: Ruby, garnet

MOON (CHANDRA)
Mantra: Om Chandraye namaha (*om chan-dra-yay nama-ha*)
Day of the Week: Monday
Colors: White, silver
Vedic Deities: Parvati, Lakshmi, Shiva
Ritual Items: Water, rice
Gems: Pearl

MARS (MANGALA)
Mantra: Om Mangalaye namaha (*om mang-ga-la-yay nama-ha*)
Day of the Week: Tuesday
Colors: Red, maroon
Vedic Deities: Kartikeya, Hanuman, Durga
Ritual Items: Red vermillion (kumkum)
Gems: Red coral

MERCURY (BUDHA)
Mantra: Om Budhaye namaha (*om bood-ha-yay nama-ha*)
Day of the Week: Wednesday
Colors: Green
Vedic Deities: Vishnu, Buddha, Saraswati
Ritual Items: Mantras, bells
Gems: Emerald, jade, turquoise

JUPITER (GURU OR BRIHASPATI)
Mantra: Om Gurave namaha (*om gura-vay nama-ha*)
Day of the Week: Thursday
Colors: Orange, yellow
Vedic Deity: Ganesh
Ritual Items: Turmeric, ghee, sweets
Gems: Yellow sapphire, yellow topaz, citrine

VENUS (SHUKRA)

Mantra: Om Shukraye Namaha (*om shook-ra-yay nama-ha*)
Day of the Week: Friday
Colors: Pink
Vedic Deities: Lakshmi, Saraswati
Ritual Items: Flowers, food, coins
Gems: Diamond, rose quartz

SATURN (SHANI)

Mantra: Om Shanaischaraya namaha (*om shan-ace-cha-rye-ya nama-ha*)
Day of the Week: Saturday
Colors: Black, dark blue
Vedic Deities: Shiva, Hanuman
Ritual Items: Sesame seeds, bare feet, camphor
Gems: Blue sapphire, lapis lazuli

RAHU

Mantra: Om Rahave namaha (*Om ra-ha-vay nama-ha*)
Day of the Week: Saturday
Colors: Brown, black, purple, dark gray, multicolored (variegated) patterns
Vedic Deities: Durga, Kali
Ritual Items: Incense (especially nag champa), sandalwood, coconuts
Gems: Hessonite

KETU

Mantra: Om Ketave namaha (*om kay-ta-vay nama-ha*)
Day of the Week: Tuesday
Colors: Beige, light gray, ash white
Vedic Deity: Ganesh
Ritual Item: Ash
Gems: Cat's eye

Glossary of Sanskrit Terms

acharya—a spiritual teacher; a learned person

Aditi—the wife of Sage Kashyapa and mother of Surya

Aditya—a name for the Sun meaning *son of Aditi*

Angiras—the son of Brahma; one of the seven rishis; father of Brihaspati

ashtanga—the eight limbs of yoga, including yama, niyama, asana, pranayama, pratyahara, dharana, dhyana, samadhi

Asura—a fallen one; given to lust, greed, and materialism

Ayurveda—the mind-body medicine system of ancient India

Bhakti Yoga—the path of devotion

Bhomaye—a name for Mars meaning *son of Mother Earth*

Bhoomi Ma—Mother Earth

Brahma—one of the three main Vedic deities; known as the Creator

Brihaspati—a personification of the planet Jupiter; priest and ritual master of the gods; senior advisor of the court; son of Angiras; also called Guru

Buddha—the enlightened being who founded Buddhism; formerly a prince

Budha—a personification of the planet Mercury; young prince of the court; illegitimate child of Tara and Chandra; adopted son of Guru

Chandra—a personification of the Moon; queen of the court

Chaya—the shadow of Samjna; shadow wife of Surya

chayagraha—shadow planets

Chitragupta—the celestial karmic accountant; works for Shani

Daksha Prajapati—the son of Brahma; held a fire ceremony where Shiva was not invited; father of Sati

Deva—a deity (*devi* is the feminine form); the gods

Dhanus—the sign of Sagittarius; an archer's bow

Dhanvantari—the god of Ayurveda, the mind-body medicine system of India

dharma—divine cosmic law

Durga—a powerful goddess symbolizing overcoming dark forces

Ganesh—an elephant-headed deity worshipped as a remover of obstacles

Gayatri—a feminine solar deity; goddess of the Vedas; consort of Brahma

Gayatri Mantra—a powerful mantra to the glory of the Sun and light

graha—meaning *to grasp*; the term for a planet

Guru—see *Brihaspati*

guru—a teacher or wise person

Halahala—a poison that arose from the churning of the ocean

Hanuman—a monkey warrior deity; symbolizes strength, service, and devotion

Jnana Yoga—the path of knowledge

Jyotish—Vedic astrology

jyotishi—a Vedic astrologer

Kali—a fierce goddess who removes the darkness of ego and ignorance

Kanya—the sign of Virgo; a young maiden

kapha—the Ayurvedic mind-body constitution related to earth

karana sharira—the causal body layer of a human being

Karkata—the sign of Cancer; a crab

Karma Yoga—the path of service and work

Kartikeya—a warrior deity related to Mars

Kashyapa—one of the seven rishis of the *Rigveda*; son of Brahma; father of Surya; husband of Aditi

Ketu—a shadow planet in Vedic astrology; south lunar node; renunciate of the court

Krishna—an incarnation of Vishnu; god of compassion, protection, and love

Kumbha—the sign of Aquarius; a water pot

lagna—the rising sign; the First House

Lakshmi—the goddess of wealth and prosperity; consort of Vishnu

Makara—the sign of Capricorn; a crocodile

Mangala—a personification of the planet Mars; commander-in-chief of the court

mantra—a sound combination used to evoke specific subtle energies

Mesha—the sign of Aries; a ram

Mina—the sign of Pisces; twin fish

Mithuna—the sign of Gemini; a couple embracing

Mohini—a feminine form of Vishnu who lured the Asuras away from the nectar of immortality

moksha—enlightenment; the goal of spiritual practices

navagraha—the nine planets of Vedic astrology

navagraha mantra—a mantra seeking the blessings of the nine planets

Neelkanth—a form of Shiva who is blue from the neck up after holding the Halahala poison in his throat

Parvati—a reincarnation of the goddess Sati; first student of yoga; wife of Shiva; mother of Ganesh

pitta—the Ayurvedic mind-body constitution related to heat

prana—vital life force

Rahu—a shadow planet in Vedic astrology; north lunar node; outlaw of the court

Raja Yoga—the path of practices and techniques

Rigveda—one of the earliest and most sacred texts of the Vedic system rishi—one of the ancient sages or seers; a source of Vedic knowledge

Samjna—the wife of Surya

Saraswati—the goddess of education, learning, and knowledge; consort of Brahma

Sati—the wife of Shiva; daughter of Daksha Prajapati

Shani—a personification of the planet Saturn; servant of the court; son of Surya; boss of Chitragupta; brother of Yama

Shiva—one of the three main Hindu deities; god of destruction and renewal; original practitioner of yoga

Shukra—a personification of the planet Venus; diplomatic advisor to the court; teacher to the Asuras

Simha—the sign of Leo; a lion

sthula sharira—the physical body layer of a human being

sukshma sharira—the subtle body layer of a human being

Surya—a personification of the Sun; king of the court

Surya Namaskar—a series of twelve yoga poses performed along with twelve solar mantras in homage to Surya

Svarbhanu—an Asura who partook of the nectar of immortality in a version of the Rahu-Ketu mythology

Tara—the wife of Brihaspati

tara—a star

Taraka—the evil Asura defeated by Kartikeya

Tula—the sign of Libra; a weighing scale

Varuna—the god of the oceans and waters; consort of Varuni

Varuni—the goddess of wine; consort of Varuna

Vasuki—the Asura serpent coiled around Shiva's neck

vata—the Ayurvedic mind-body constitution related to air

Vedas—original texts of ancient Vedic tradition

Vedic knowledge system—the vast knowledge framework of ancient India

Vishnu—one of the three main Hindu deities; god of maintenance and preservation

Vishvakarma—the celestial architect who reduced Surya's intensity

Vrishabha—the sign of Taurus; a bull

Vrishchika—the sign of Scorpio; a scorpion

Yama—the lord of death and dharma; brother of Shani

yama—a set of guidelines for personal disciplines; first limb of eight limbs of Raja Yoga

yoga—a system of spiritual self-development

Bibliography

Behari, Bepin. *Myths & Symbols of Vedic Astrology*. 2nd ed. Twin Lakes, Wis.: Lotus, 2003.

Chatterji, Vish and Yogrishi Vishvketu. *The Business Casual Yogi: Take Charge of Your Body, Mind, and Career*. San Rafael, Calif.: Mandala, 2019.

Frawley, David. *Astrology of the Seers: A Guide to Vedic/Hindu Astrology*. Twin Lakes, Wis.: Lotus, 2000.

Mani, Vettam. *Puranic Encyclopaedia*. 11th ed. Delhi: Motilal Banarsidass, 2021.

Radhe [Susan Pfau]. *Your Healing Stars*. Vol. 1, *Fundamentals of Vedic Astrology*. Charleston, S. C.: Shree Ganapati Productions, 2016.

Rao, V. S. *Navagraha Purana: Tales of the Nine Planets*. 9th ed. Edited by Preetha Rajah Kannan. Mumbai: Jaico, 2022.

Sharma, Girish Chand. *Maharishi Parasara's Brihat Parasara Hora Sastra: A Compendium in Vedic Astrology*. Vol. 1. 5th ed. New Delhi: Sagar, 2006.

About the Author

After a successful career as an engineer, executive, and entrepreneur, Vish Chatterji is honoring his soul purpose as an East-meets-West executive coach. He helps leaders find light in their work through leveraging the wisdom of yoga, meditation, Ayurveda (mind-body medicine), and Jyotish (karmic advising).

Vish holds a BS in mechanical engineering from Northwestern University, an MBA from the University of Michigan, and an executive coaching certificate from UC Berkeley. Vish has studied in traditional Himalayan ashrams and at the Chopra Center for Wellbeing in California, and he teaches globally.

Vish served as a board director for the Beach Cities Health District in Los Angeles County and is the co-author of *The Business Casual Yogi: Take Charge of Your Body, Mind, and Career*, also published by Mandala. He is a married father of three and loves to garden, bicycle, and fix things around the house.

Website: headandheartinsights.com

MANDALA

An imprint of MandalaEarth
PO Box 3088
San Rafael, CA 94912
www.MandalaEarth.com

Publisher Raoul Goff
Associate Publisher Phillip Jones
Publishing Director Katie Killebrew
Editor Peter Adrian Behravesh
Editorial Assistant Amanda Nelson
VP Creative Director Chrissy Kwasnik
Art Director Ashley Quackenbush
Senior Designer Stephanie Odeh
VP Manufacturing Alix Nicholaeff
Senior Production Manager Joshua Smith
Sr Production Manager, Subsidiary Rights Lina s Palma-Temena

MandalaEarth would also like to thank Bob Cooper and Jessica Easto.

Text © 2024 Vish Chatterji
Foreword © 2024 Sheila Patel, MD

ISBN: 979-8-88762-102-9

Manufactured in Turkey by Insight Editions

10 9 8 7 6 5 4 3 2 1

The information provided in this book is strictly for reference only and is not in any manner a substitute for medical advice or direct guidance from a qualified professional.

Insight Editions, in association with Roots of Peace, will plant two trees for each tree used in the manufacturing of this book. Roots of Peace is an internationally renowned humanitarian organization dedicated to eradicating land mines worldwide and converting war-torn lands into productive farms and wildlife habitats. Roots of Peace will plant two million fruit and nut trees in Afghanistan and provide farmers there with the skills and support necessary for sustainable land use.

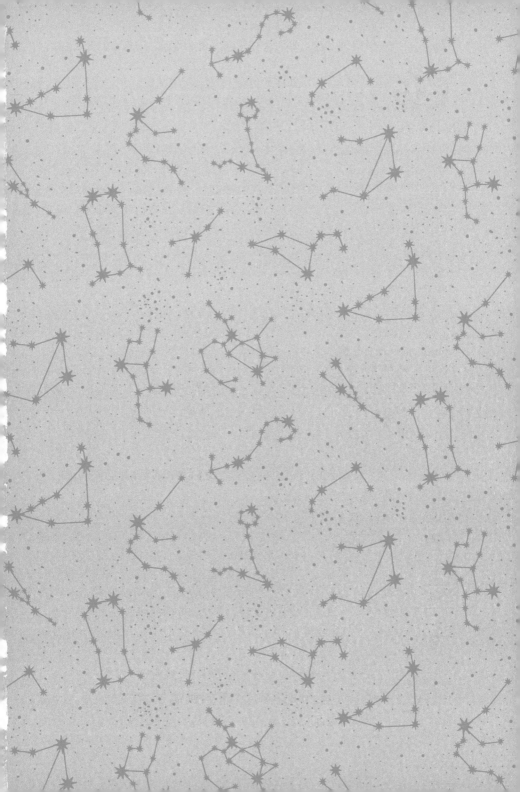

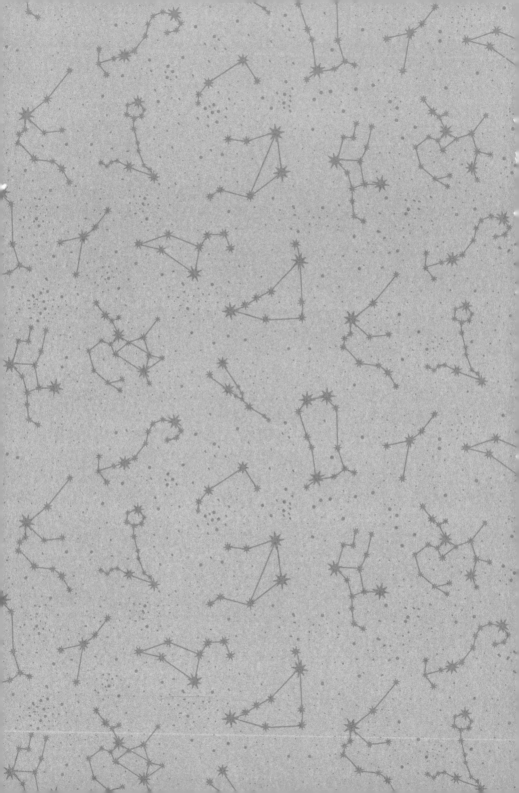